THE BOOK OF

MASSIVELY EPIC ENGINEERING DISASTERS

THE BOOK OF

MASSIVELY EPIC
ENGINEERING
DISASTERS

SEAN CONNOLLY

WORKMAN PUBLISHING • NEW YORK

Library of Congress Cataloging-in-Publication Data is available.

ISBN 978-0-7611-8394-5

Design by Galen Smith
Cover by Galen Smith
Cover and interior illustrations by Pat Lewis
Editing by Danny Cooper
Production editing by Beth Levy
Photo research by Angela Cherry
Production manager: Steven Bucsok

Photo credits appear on page 241.

Workman books are available at special discounts when purchased in bulk for premiums and sales promotions as well as for fund-raising or educational use. Special editions or book excerpts can also be created to specification. For details, contact the Special Sales Director at the address below, or send an email to specialmarkets@workman.com.

Workman Publishing Co., Inc.
225 Varick Street
New York, NY 10014-4381
workman.com

WORKMAN is a registered trademark of Workman Publishing Co., Inc.

Printed in the United States of America

First printing July 2017

10 9 8 7 6 5 4 3 2 1

To the memory of my parents,
who laid a solid foundation and
gave me the tools to help me through life.

A famous song contains the lyrics "What a long, strange trip it's been." Those words could have described the journey that writing this book has taken, lasting about 2,000 years (okay—*covering* about 2,000 years) and calling at temples, stadiums, battlefields, and disappearing lakes along the way.

A trip like that needs good guides, and I'm indebted to the planners, engineers, and builders whose successes and failures inspired this book. Without studying and learning from their work, I'd never have had the material to fill these pages.

On a more practical note, those typed pages would never have become the printed pages you read without the help of my "team of experts." They include my agent, Jim Levine of the Levine Greenberg Rostan Literary Agency; and Workman Publishing's two "Daniels": Daniel Nayeri, Director of Children's Publishing, and the indefatigable editor Danny Cooper. Special thanks also go out to Galen Smith for the lively and pleasing design, and diligent production editor Beth Levy for her keen eye.

In addition, the following individuals and organizations have provided inspiration or assistance, and sometimes both: Berkshire Film & Video, Nicholas Brakspear, Frank Ciccotti, Christopher Edwards, Gregory Etter, Dr. Sally Heneghan, Gary Hoffman, Kingswood School, Dr. Peter Lydon, M.I.T.'s Educational Studies Program, Robert Rauch, Peter Rielly, Jennifer Spohn, and Elizabeth Stell.

CONTENTS

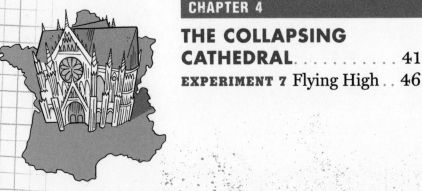

Introduction x

CHAPTER 1

THE COLOSSUS OF RHODES 1
EXPERIMENT 1 All Shook Up 6
EXPERIMENT 2 Hold That Pose 10

CHAPTER 2

FIDENAE STADIUM COLLAPSES 15
EXPERIMENT 3 From the Ground Up 20
EXPERIMENT 4 Weighing the Possibilities 24

CHAPTER 3

THE LEANING TOWER OF PISA 29
EXPERIMENT 5 Will It Tip? 34
EXPERIMENT 6 It's Sinking In 36

CHAPTER 4

THE COLLAPSING CATHEDRAL 41
EXPERIMENT 7 Flying High .. 46

CHAPTER 5

THE TAY BRIDGE DISASTER 49
EXPERIMENT 8 Wind Load 54
EXPERIMENT 9 Snap, Crackle 58

CHAPTER 6

THE "UNSINKABLE" *TITANIC* 61
EXPERIMENT 10 Staying Afloat 66
EXPERIMENT 11 Overflow! 70

CHAPTER 7

THE BOSTON MOLASSES FLOOD 75
EXPERIMENT 12 Holding Up to Pressure 80
EXPERIMENT 13 Slow as Molasses? 84

CHAPTER 8

THE *HINDENBURG* CRASHES 87
EXPERIMENT 14 Don't Give Me Static 92
EXPERIMENT 15 Down in Flames 95

CHAPTER 9

THE TACOMA NARROWS BRIDGE 99
EXPERIMENT 16 Damping Tactics 104

CHAPTER 10

SHERMAN TANKS GET STUCK 109
EXPERIMENT 17 Elephant's Footprint 114

CHAPTER 11

FLIGHT OF THE "SPRUCE GOOSE" 119
EXPERIMENT 18 Pressure Drop 124
EXPERIMENT 19 "Drag" Racing 127

CHAPTER 12

THE PLYWOOD SKYSCRAPER 131
EXPERIMENT 20 Blowing Hot and Cold 136
EXPERIMENT 21 Into the Swing 140

CHAPTER 13

RADIAL TIRES COME UNGLUED 145
EXPERIMENT 22 Corrosion Damage 150
EXPERIMENT 23 Spinning Out 154

CHAPTER 14

WHOOPS—THE LAKE'S GONE 159
EXPERIMENT 24 The Violent Vortex 164

CHAPTER 15

THE SINCLAIR C5 STALLS 169
EXPERIMENT 25 Taking Things Wide 174
EXPERIMENT 26 Onward and Upward? 178

CHAPTER 16

THE *EXXON VALDEZ* OIL SPILL 183
EXPERIMENT 27 Double Hulls 188

CHAPTER 17

THE PARIS AIRPORT COLLAPSE 193
EXPERIMENT 28 Metal Expansion 198

CHAPTER 18

CHILE'S TRAPPED MINERS 201
EXPERIMENT 29 Stay on Target 206

CHAPTER 19

THE METRODOME DEFLATES 211
EXPERIMENT 30 The Pressure's On 216
EXPERIMENT 31 Why a Dome? 219

CHAPTER 20

THE INFAMOUS "FRYSCRAPER" 223
EXPERIMENT 32 Reflect or Absorb? 228
EXPERIMENT 33 The Umbrella Oven 232

Afterword 237

At a Glance 238

INTRODUCTION

"THAT'S A GREAT TOWER

you've built! Just the right height, pretty arches, and that white marble really shows it off. Just one itty-bitty thing—that lean. It really does tilt, and people are even beginning to call it the Leaning Tower of Pisa."

"Oh, that? Don't worry! It's just settling in. Give it a year or two and it will straighten out."

You can imagine this conversation taking place back in the Middle Ages, when work was finally finished on the bell tower of Pisa Cathedral. Centuries have passed, and the tower still leans worryingly. But with better planning, mainly in the engineering department, the famous tower would never have tilted in the first place.

HOW BAD IS BAD?

Could you really call the Leaning Tower an engineering disaster? You could even argue the opposite—that it put Pisa on the international tourist map. After all, who goes out of their way to see the Upright Tower of Bologna or the Perpendicular Column of Naples? But in the end, there's something a bit . . . embarrassing . . . about that tower in Pisa.

It's not the only "whoops" example that you'll get a chance to examine in *The Book of Massively Epic Engineering Disasters*. How about that open-top electric vehicle, the Sinclair C5, that was launched *in the rain* on a winter afternoon? Or the "Spruce Goose," one of the

largest and most expensive planes ever built, which had just one flight and reached an altitude of—wait for it—70 feet? Or maybe the Louisiana lake that just drained away like an emptying bathtub because oil engineers drilled through the wrong bit of lake bed?

All of those seem almost comical and harmless, but engineering mistakes can also lead to deadly consequences. Thousands died when a hastily constructed wooden coliseum collapsed nearly 2,000 years ago in Italy. The catastrophic loss of the *Titanic* in 1912 can be traced to poor engineering as well. Even Boston's deadly Molasses (yes, molasses) Flood of 1919 could have been prevented if engineers had paid more attention to the way liquids behave under enormous pressure.

ASKING THE RIGHT QUESTIONS

In the following pages, you'll be able to examine 20 engineering disasters from ancient times right up to the 21st century. Pay attention, because you've been called in to make sure these mistakes don't happen again!

A brief introduction to each episode sets the stage, locking it into a time and place so you can get a feel for what happened when disaster struck. Then you have a chance to look more closely in the section called "What Went Wrong?" That's where you get the full story, including the consequences—and cost—of each engineering mishap.

Armed with that information, you can try to "Turn Back the Clock." And that's where the fun really begins.

Here's where you go behind the scenes to find out not just *what* happened in each case, but *why* it happened. And that "why," more often than not, is down to engineering. You'll see how things could have been changed or considered differently at every stage of development. These are the sort of concerns that engineers deal with every day.

Engineering, of course, is all about getting things made and operating well. But it's also about using your curiosity along the way and asking questions. A successful project has a lot of "what ifs," "how abouts," and "why nots" built into it. This section of the book is your chance to examine some of these questions . . . because you'll be asking more of your own in the final section of each chapter. And you might be surprised by some of the answers.

OVER TO YOU

Each chapter has one or two experiments to help drive home the scientific principle that had a starring role in the disaster. You could find yourself experimenting with air pressure, thermal stress, the center of mass, or seismic waves. There's even a great experiment to demonstrate non-Newtonian liquids, but fair warning: You might wind up with toothpaste on the ceiling!

YOU WILL NEED
All the stuff you need to perform the experiment is listed in this section. You'll find nearly everything around your house, in the garage, or in a shed.

METHOD
The instructions on how to conduct the experiment are numbered clearly and as easy to follow as a cooking recipe or instructions for building a model.

WHAT'S UP?

Here's your chance to make the connection between the experiment you've just conducted and the main scientific principles at work.

TAKE CARE!

Every now and then an experiment will have a warning to make sure that you're careful about flames, sharp objects, or other potential risks.

BACK TO THE DRAWING BOARD?

Remember that *The Book of Massively Epic Engineering Disasters* is all about getting to the root of what went wrong and how things could have been engineered differently to avoid disaster. With your own smarts, new scientific knowledge, and firsthand experience, you'll be in a lucky position.

Now, *there's* something you can build on!

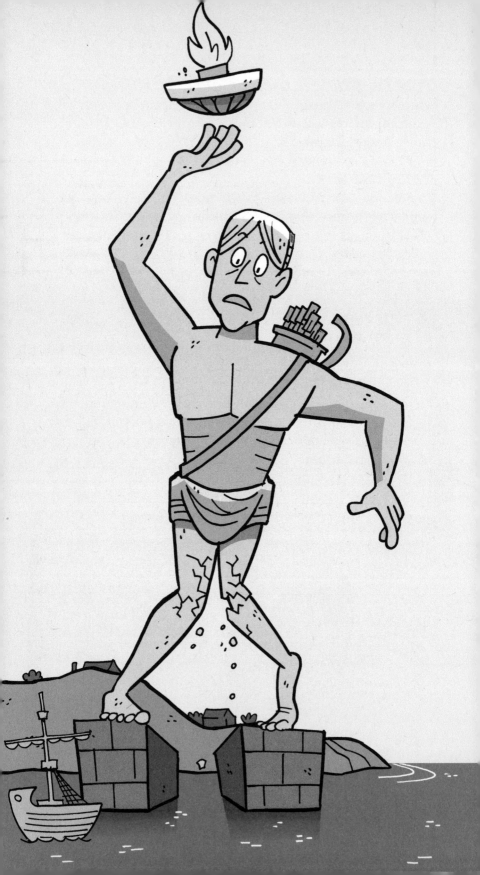

CHAPTER 1

THE COLOSSUS OF RHODES

Your pulse quickens as you stand on deck and see land, and then the outline of a city. That city, with its breathtaking skyscrapers, is already familiar to you—even though you have never been there. The soaring towers and "concrete canyons" are unmistakable: You are arriving in New York City. And any doubts you might have had are swept away as you pass the towering figure of a robed lady holding a torch aloft.

That world-famous guardian to New York Harbor is, of course, the Statue of Liberty. Towering 150 feet above a base just as high, she is the powerful symbol of America and its freedom.

This majestic lady goes by another name: the "New Colossus." The original Colossus—every bit as tall—guarded the entrance to the harbor of Rhodes, an island in the Mediterranean Sea. The Colossus of Rhodes was built more than 2,000 years ago and stood for more than 60 years until it came tumbling down in an earthquake in 226 BC. But could the ancient engineers have done anything to protect that Wonder of the Ancient World?

WHAT WENT WRONG?

THE GREEK ISLAND of Rhodes lies at the eastern end of the Mediterranean Sea, just off the coast of what is now called Turkey. When Alexander the Great conquered the island in 332 BC, the Rhodians (inhabitants of Rhodes) welcomed him and his Greek way of life. After Alexander died in 323 BC, they joined Egypt in supporting one of his generals, Ptolemy, in a lengthy civil war. In 305 BC, Ptolemy's archrival, Antigonus, sent his son Demetrius to conquer Rhodes. Demetrius's 40,000 soldiers had a huge portable tower to attack the walls of Rhodes, but a sudden storm destroyed it. The Rhodians then flooded the path of a second mega-tower so that the tower tipped over in the mud.

With ships soon to arrive from Egypt to help Rhodes, Demetrius decided to make his getaway. The people of Rhodes believed that they owed their victory to their patron god, Helios. What better way to commemorate the victory than to build a huge statue of Helios guarding the island harbor just as he had guarded the islanders in battle?

It's most likely that work began on the Colossus in 292 BC and continued for 12 years. The "skeleton" of the statue was made of iron bars, with bronze plates forming the "skin." It stood on a 60-foot-wide marble pedestal. The bronze plates were

THE SEVEN WONDERS OF THE WORLD

Travelers in ancient times included the Colossus of Rhodes among the Seven Wonders of the World, each of them a marvel of human design and engineering. The others are:

- The Pyramids of Giza (Egypt)
- The Hanging Gardens of Babylon (Iraq)
- The Temple of Artemis at Ephesus (Turkey)
- The Statue of Zeus (Greece)
- The Mausoleum at Halicarnassus (Turkey)
- The Lighthouse of Alexandria (Egypt)

about 5-feet square, with turned-in edges so they could be riveted together.

The finished statue stood magnificently above the entrance to the harbor at Rhodes—just as "Lady Liberty" guards New York Harbor. It looked set to loom over Rhodes for centuries. Except it didn't—it fell in 226 BC, when Rhodes suffered a terrible earthquake. Many buildings and temples were destroyed, and accounts tell us that the Colossus snapped at its knees and toppled to the ground in pieces. All we have now are the fragments that lay for centuries alongside the harbor.

TURN BACK THE CLOCK

IT'S A BIT UNFAIR FOR modern engineers to look back more than 2,000 years and pick holes in construction techniques that people used. After all, ancient people had no electricity or power tools of any type. Plus, we can only estimate the full size of the Colossus by "back-engineering"—working out the full size of the statue by examining measurements of a thumb or nose fragment. These lead to the conclusion that the Colossus really was colossal. So how can we claim to know any better about making it stand up to the test of time?

Well, one word tells us everything about why the Colossus toppled and lots about how modern engineers approach the same problem: earthquake. It was that single event, probably only lasting a few minutes, that spelled the end of the Colossus. People in the Mediterranean region were no strangers to earthquakes, yet they continued to build structures that would snap and topple rather than sway and remain upright.

WHAT CAUSES EARTHQUAKES?

The outer layer of the Earth, called the crust, isn't one continuous piece of solid rock. It's more like a jigsaw puzzle of different pieces, called plates. The joints between plates are known as faults, and that's where most earthquakes occur. Two neighboring plates might move smoothly along each other until one of them catches and sticks while it's still being forced from behind. Eventually it causes the plates to suddenly judder—just as your foot judders if you use it to stop when you're on your bike.

Modern engineers working in known earthquake zones such as Tokyo or San Francisco design buildings to withstand a great deal of earthquake force. Much of the damage comes from the ground's swaying back and forth in an earthquake, so architects add dampers (like a car's shock absorbers) to absorb the lateral (back-and-forth) force. The building above is far less affected. Other techniques boil down to common sense—new buildings use lighter materials, especially on the roof. Just think: Would you like to be living beneath a heavy concrete roof if the walls under it started swaying in an earthquake?

But were those early engineers really so ignorant of solutions to deal with earthquakes? Think of some of the other statues from thousands of years ago. The Great Sphinx in Egypt lies there eternally. The Statue of Zeus, seated on a throne in Olympia, Greece, lasted about 1,000 years through several earthquakes until fire destroyed its wooden frame. The seated "pose" of these statues—with weight spread out along the base—was very different from that of the Colossus, with only its two feet supporting its weight.

ALL SHOOK UP

This experiment gives you a taste (well, maybe the "taste" comes after the experiment) of how building designers test things out against known forces. New buildings in Tokyo and San Francisco are built to hold up well against different earthquake forces. You can see how engineers have worked out those designs with this tabletop experiment.

YOU WILL NEED

> Jell-O mix (about five 16-ounce packs)
> Water
> Three 8½- x 11-inch disposable baking pans (at least 2½ inches deep)
> Toothpicks (at least 120)
> 3 friends
> Miniature marshmallows (about 2 packs)

METHOD

1 The night before, mix up enough Jell-O with water to fill the three baking pans. Let them cool in the refrigerator overnight.

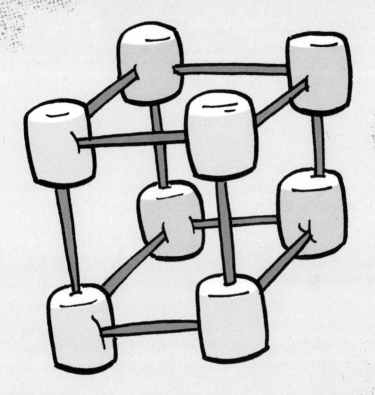

2 Divide the toothpicks among three people.

3 Have each person insert the toothpicks into the marshmallows and form squares, cubes, and triangles out of them so that the marshmallows become the "joints." (If you like, you can add diagonal braces within these structures.)

4 Add extra floors to the structures by connecting toothpicks from the new floor through the marshmallow corners. See how tall a building each person can construct.

CONTINUED

5 Place each building on a Jell-O tray.

6 Shake the tray back and forth evenly to re-create S waves (the back-and-forth waves that earthquakes cause).

7 Compare each design—did any survive the earthquake? How tall or wide can a building be made from the same amount of toothpicks?

WHAT'S UP?

This experiment is a home-lab version of what seismic (earthquake) engineers do when they test building designs to stand up to earthquake forces. Powerful bursts of energy, known as seismic waves, travel through the layers of the Earth, causing vibrations. Some of those vibrations are powerful enough to break the layers, causing earthquakes.

Of course, life would be easier if everyone lived in one-story houses spread along the ground—and you might have seen how those withstand the earthquake forces. But most cities are crowded, and we must build upward, sometimes dozens of stories high. If engineers can find a way to overcome similar vibrations in Jell-O models (or their own lab equivalents), they can use those lessons in real design.

HOLD THAT POSE

Have you ever wondered why the Statue of Liberty wears that flowing robe and isn't standing there in a softball uniform, bathing suit, or some other outfit that shows her two legs supporting her? There's certainly an artistic reason, of course. She looks nobler in that robe—reminding us of the ideals of liberty and democracy that go back to Ancient Greece (where lots of people wore those robes).

Her robe also serves a practical purpose. The folds look loose and light, but they're as solid as everything else in the statue, and they go right down to the base. Are you beginning to get the picture? Here's your chance to be a sculptor, and to see how the pose you choose might really be a sensible engineering decision.

YOU WILL NEED

> **Willing volunteers (at least 3)**
> **Slippery floor (polished wood or tile)**
> **Light rug**
> **Light wooden chair**

TAKE CARE!

You'll need to do this experiment in a clear, open space so there's nothing that your "statue" could hit if he or she loses their balance.

METHOD

1 Explain that you're looking for the best possible pose for a sculpture to stand up better than the Colossus of Rhodes.

2 Have one friend stand with feet together on the rug.

3 Let the others help you give one end of the rug a good tug.

4 See whether your "statue" has remained upright.

CONTINUED

5 Try the same methods (using the same volunteer for scientific accuracy) with a different pose: still standing, but with feet wide apart.

6 Repeat Steps 3 and 4.

7 Now have your model sit on the chair and repeat Steps 3 and 4.

WHAT'S UP?

This experiment probably generated a few laughs, but it also demonstrates an important engineering principle. An object such as a statue or building will be more stable if its weight is spread along a wide base. The first pose concentrated the volunteer's weight on a small area—his two feet held close together. The second widened that area, probably making him more secure, and the final pose (like Zeus in the ancient statue) transferred the weight to an even wider area. So if Helios had been seated on a throne rather than standing upright, maybe he'd still be guarding Rhodes.

FIDENAE STADIUM COLLAPSES

There's nothing the ancient Romans liked more than the brutal theater of the gladiatorial games. That is, *most* Romans. Emperor Tiberius, one of Rome's most successful generals, who ruled the Empire for over two decades, hated watching gladiators fight to the death in Rome's Colosseum. In fact, he didn't even like Rome that much, and spent his last years on the island of Capri. With the grouchy emperor—and his ban on "games"—out of the picture, fun-loving Romans rushed to make up for lost time.

By AD 27 a new stadium—a wooden version of the Colosseum—had been built just outside Rome, in the town of Fidenae. Up to 50,000 spectators crammed into it on the opening day, expecting life-or-death struggles to be played out before them. Instead, the deaths came in the stands. The hastily built stadium, which was dangerously overloaded, collapsed. Up to 20,000 people died as a result, making it the deadliest stadium accident in history.

WHAT WENT WRONG?

ANYONE WHO'S EVER seen the majestic Colosseum or any of the other ancient monuments scattered across Rome will figure that those guys knew how to build things to last. Sure, some of these structures are in ruins, but what do you expect after 2,000 years of invasions, rebellions, and looting? Well, the Fidenae Stadium collapse might make you think differently— it seems people were out to make a "quick buck" off crummy buildings even in ancient times. A former slave named Atilius saw a chance to host gladiatorial games once Tiberius's ban ended, and he cashed in quickly by building a new stadium close to Rome.

The Colosseum and other major stadiums were made of a mixture of concrete and stone, giving them strength and durability. Those are expensive materials, so Atilius chose to cut corners and build his stadium from wood— a cheap alternative, but not as strong. Atilius also never worked out (or simply ignored) the limit of spectators that the stadium structure could hold safely. Worse still, the stadium had little or no foundation to support it.

WHY SO POPULAR?

Why were Romans so eager to watch "the games"? The largest stadiums, such as the Colosseum, provided daylong performances of wild animals—including lions and hyenas shipped in from Africa—fighting each other or attacking criminals. Gladiators battled one another using a variety of weapons and defenses, including clubs, lances, swords, and nets. And if the Emperor was watching, a contest could be suspended with a sword pointing down at a crouching victim. Would the Emperor spare the gladiator's life, or would he give the thumbs-down sign?

The cards were stacked against those 50,000 fans. All walks of life were present—merchants, fishermen, winemakers, and wealthy landowners. Mingling with them were eager boys and girls, and even grandmothers. The Roman writer Tacitus noted that these people were "starved for gladiatorial presentations," so it's not surprising that they jumped at the chance to see their favorite entertainment as soon as it was available. Once inside the stadium, the heaving thousands noticed an ominous swaying. Then the stadium fell in on itself, collapsing both inward and outward and crushing thousands.

Nearly 1,800 years later, it's clear that the stadium was doomed. Poor materials, bad planning, and no foundation are on the major no-no list for any respectable architect, engineer, or builder!

TURN BACK THE CLOCK

"PUBLIC SAFETY" sounds about as exciting as watching paint dry, but the term applies to planning, design, and regulations to make sure that you can do everyday things that *are* exciting—ride on a subway or bus, buy hot dogs from a stand, or attend a ball game—without fear of being injured. The way we look at public buildings, like sports stadiums, is based on the principle of public safety.

A modern sports stadium has lots of features that the Colosseum or the Fidenae Stadium lacked—electronic scoreboards, sound systems, and maybe a retractable roof—but the structure is remarkably similar. Most are shaped like bowls, with rows of seats ranged on a slope leading up from the field. So the same basic principles of safe construction apply.

ALLOY

A metal made by melting two metals (or a metal and a nonmetal) and mixing them together to preserve the properties of both ingredients, such as hardness or flexibility.

Any large building needs to rest on a sound foundation. It must be deep enough to provide stability and to absorb the weight of the building (and people) above it. The construction materials are also important. Modern stadiums use steel and metal alloys to provide strength; the Colosseum builders used stone and concrete. Wood is a bad choice—it's weaker and burns easily.

Just as important, though, are the calculations to work out how much force all those thousands of spectators would exert on the structure. Designers alter the design once they have worked out spectator numbers—they might sacrifice capacity (number of seats) to make sure that they stay within safe limits. Most of those basic principles were familiar to Roman engineers, and the Roman senate even produced strict building regulations after the Fidenae disaster.

BETTER LATE THAN NEVER

The war-waging Romans were no strangers to death on a large scale, but even they were horrified by the destruction at Fidenae. The Senate responded by producing what we would now call building regulations. Most important, the rules insisted that any new public building be constructed on firm ground with a good foundation. Next they decreed that no one with a fortune of less than 400,000 sesteres (about $700,000 in today's money) be allowed to construct public buildings—sorry, Atilius.

FROM THE GROUND UP

You've probably been in basements loads of times—maybe at your school, in a library, or just at a friend's house. But have you ever wondered why each of those buildings even has a basement, aside from needing extra space for a Ping-Pong table, washer-dryer, and those old Halloween costumes and rusty skates you've never managed to throw away?

Well, basements occupy the space created inside the walls of an important feature: the foundation. The floor beneath the ground level (the foundation) captures and spreads the force of the building outward. If the building just rested on the ground, there would be nothing to stop that force from toppling the building. But the ground on either side of the foundation resists that destabilizing force, making the building more secure and stable.

YOU WILL NEED

- ➤ **Modeling clay (or play dough)**
- ➤ **3 chopsticks**
- ➤ **Bucket (about 1-foot diameter opening)**
- ➤ **Sand**
- ➤ **6 paperback books (or more)**
- ➤ **Ruler**

METHOD

1 Form the clay into 6 balls, each about the size of a grape, and stick 1 clay ball onto each end of the 3 chopsticks.

2 Fill the bucket with sand, leaving 2 to 3 inches clear of sand at the top.

3 Rest the chopsticks upright on the sand so that the bases form a triangle (with the clay balls almost touching each other).

4 Carefully lay a book on the platform that the clay balls at the top have made.

CONTINUED

5 If the tower still stands, add another book and continue until the tower tips over, noting how many books you can stack.

6 Now form a similar triangle-shaped arrangement but with the clay balls buried under an inch of sand.

7 Repeat Steps 4 and 5.

8 Finally, bury the clay balls 4 inches under the sand and repeat Steps 4 and 5.

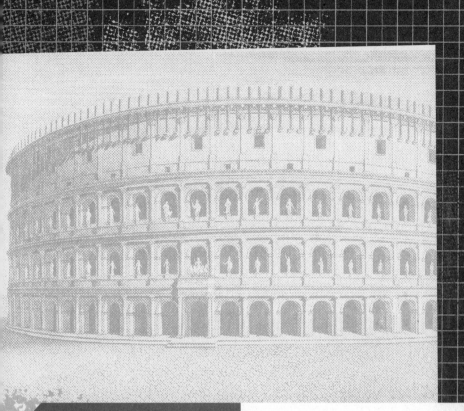

WHAT'S UP?

The downward force of the book was enough to topple the shallow foundation when the "towers" were resting on the sand. Some of that force pushed sand from around the foundation. As the foundation got deeper and wider, more and more force was needed to topple it, largely because the depth of the sand surrounding the foundation called for more force to move it. The deeper the foundation, the more secure the building above it.

WEIGHING THE POSSIBILITIES

Ancient Roman engineers had plenty of common sense and hard-won experience, but the "quick buck" building approach used for the Fidenae Stadium was a different matter. Atilius's builders failed to work out how much weight the wooden levels of the stadium itself could hold. (You may have seen "Maximum Load" warnings inside an elevator.)

This experiment gives you a chance to work out something that the stadium builders at Fidenae overlooked: load capacity. Getting it right means having a building that lasts through the ages. Getting it wrong can be . . . disastrous.

YOU WILL NEED

- 6 sheets of letter paper (8.5- x 11-inch)
- Clear tape
- Sharp pencil
- Styrofoam coffee cup
- String (24 inches)
- 2 paper clips
- 2 identical kitchen chairs
- Pennies (about 100)

METHOD

1 Roll up 1 sheet of paper lengthwise to make a tube and use a strip of tape at each end to keep it rolled and secure.

2 Use the pencil to poke a hole on both sides of the cup, about an inch down from the rim.

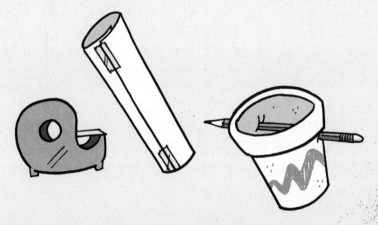

3 Cut a length of string about 2 feet long and tie a paper clip to one end.

4 Feed the free end of the string through both holes of the cup and then tie a paper clip to that end.

5 Pull gently on the middle of the string so the paper clips are drawn back to the cup and you have a loop above it.

CONTINUED

6 Face the kitchen chairs toward each other, about 8 inches apart, and rest the rolled-up paper on the seats so it makes a bridge between them.

7 Lift the paper and slide the cup beneath it, so that it hangs down from the middle.

8 Try to predict how many pennies you can add to the cup before it buckles under the force (weight) of the coins.

9 Continue to add coins until it buckles and note the amount.

10 Try the same demonstration but with a double layer of paper—2 sheets rolled up lengthwise. Predict how many coins this version will hold.

11 Repeat once more with 3 sheets—have you detected a pattern?

WHAT'S UP?

You've just been doing a basic version of load-bearing calculations—just the sort of thing that could have saved thousands of lives if Atilius had bothered to do them. The paper could represent one beam of a building, and the coins could represent people. Using stronger materials (or in this case, reinforcing the paper) allows a similar length of beam to support more weight.

CHAPTER 3

THE LEANING TOWER OF PISA

Can there be anyone in the world who doesn't recognize what is probably the most famous engineering disaster of all time? Its image has appeared in movies, books, and magazines so often that it almost seems a little unreal—like a unicorn or a dragon. And when people see the Leaning Tower of Pisa in person, they're often tempted to stick around a while, just to be there when it finally *does* fall over.

But it doesn't—and it hasn't for more than 800 years. Other mistakes bite the dust within months of appearing on the world scene. The Leaning Tower of Pisa, on the other hand, just leans and leans and leans, remaining a favorite for tourists and engineers alike. Is it defying gravity? Do normal rules of science not apply? Why did it stop where it did and not tilt farther? Is it made of marshmallows or something? This very familiar building turns out to be quite a mystery after all. . . .

WHAT WENT WRONG?

THE CITY OF PISA lies on Italy's west coast, at the mouth of the River Arno. By the 12th century, Pisa had become a powerful trading, artistic, and military center. In that period, just a couple of centuries before Italy gave birth to the Renaissance, notable cities like Pisa, Florence, Venice, and others demonstrated their importance by constructing marvelous religious buildings.

In the mid-1100s, the Pisans set about building a collection of those buildings, all to be finished in brilliant white marble. The largest was the cathedral, flanked by the baptistery and the campanile (bell tower). Work on the bell tower, which was to become the most famous of the three, began in 1173. Like the other buildings, it marked the transition from the heavier Romanesque style of architecture—full of curved arches—to the lighter Gothic style, with slender columns rising high toward the heavens.

The only problem was that instead of soaring heavenward, the tower began sinking earthward. And it didn't even sink straight. First it tilted one way, and builders tried to mask the problem by building unevenly (to make it look straighter). Then it began tilting the other way, and they tried the same trick on the other side. Nothing seemed to be going right!

RENAISSANCE

A period in the late Middle Ages when Europeans rediscovered some of the artistic traditions of the ancient Greeks and Romans and began applying them to their own art, architecture, and culture.

By the 14th century, it was clear that Pisa's bell tower had a major problem. It was already known as the *Torre Pendente* (Leaning Tower). Nevertheless, work continued on the tower until it reached its full 8-story height in 1370. It was complete, but still had its tilt of about 3 degrees off vertical.

GOING, GOING, GONE!

The inhabitants of Pavia, about 125 miles north of Pisa, could have told the Pisans a thing or two about falling towers. On the morning of March 18, 1989, bricks started falling from the town's 236-foot-high Civic Tower. Within minutes, the tower simply collapsed, killing four people and injuring 15. The exact cause of the collapse is still a mystery—the tower had stood since 1060 and never even tilted.

That leaning tower eventually became world-famous—it is as recognizable as the Empire State Building or the Taj Mahal, and is the subject of thousands of joke photos each year (with people pretending to push it back). But would this beautiful example of Italian architecture be half as famous if it had turned out straight?

TURN BACK THE CLOCK

TWO BIG FACTORS almost certainly account for the famous tilt in Pisa's bell tower: unstable soil and inadequate foundations beneath the tower. Builders probably brushed aside concerns about either of these, because two large religious buildings already stood on the level ground where work began on the tower in 1173. The cathedral and baptistery are both massive structures, and their tiny tilting can't be noticed with the naked eye.

So it must have come as a shock, soon after construction began, to see the tower beginning to lean to the north when the builders had reached only the third of the planned eight stories. Despite being interrupted by numerous wars, workers undertook the 840-year process to save the tower. At first they tried optical illusions: They lengthened the columns on the north side of the third floor to make the tower look more level. By 1272, the tower was leaning to the south (the direction it still points), so builders began making the south columns longer on upper floors.

DANGEROUS DISTRACTIONS?

Italy in the Middle Ages wasn't a single, united country as it is now. Instead, it was a patchwork of city-states and small kingdoms that always seemed to be fighting each other. Pisa was at war off and on for centuries, and the tower's construction was halted and resumed several times as a result. Could that type of distraction have played a part in the whole business? Well, think of the times you've heard your parents call, "How can you do your homework with that music on?!"

It wasn't until the 20th century that engineers really got to work trying to stop the tilt—or at least protect the tower from toppling. Scientists in 1911 measured the movement of the top of the tower at 0.05 inch a year, and the rate was getting worse. After a similar tower in Pavia collapsed in 1989, the tower was closed to the public.

Scientists and engineers from around the world worked out a long-term plan, beginning in 1990, to remove soil carefully from the "high" end of the tower bit by bit. It was a complicated maneuver, but rested on the basic principle of center of mass. The tower was reopened in 2001, and engineers confidently predicted that it would be safe for the next 300 years. Time will tell. . . .

CENTER OF MASS

An imaginary point either inside an object or near it where the mass of the object could be considered to be most concentrated.

WILL IT TIP?

Remember, the scientific term "center of mass" means the point at which the mass of an object could be said to be concentrated. What does that mean? Well, in an object that has the same mass throughout—like a hockey puck—it would be right in the middle. But in a hammer, which has unevenly distributed mass, the center of mass would be way over by the head of the hammer.

Why is all this important, especially for the Tower of Pisa? Simple. If something's center of mass is within the base of the object (the part touching the ground), then the object will stay upright. If not, well, hold on tight, because it's going to tip. This experiment shows how the center of mass moves as something tips. That was happening for centuries in Pisa. Watch what happens when it goes a little too far.

YOU WILL NEED

> **Empty soda can**
> **Floor, table, or counter**
> **Water**

METHOD

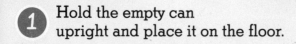

1 Hold the empty can upright and place it on the floor.

2 Tilt the can so it's resting on just a small bit of its base and let go—it will tip over.

3 Try tilting it at different angles and letting go—same result.

4 Fill the can about one-third full with water.

5 Repeat Step 3—if you're careful, the can will stay standing (and still tipped) when you remove your hand.

1/3

WHAT'S UP?

When you started out, the center of mass for the empty can was pretty much in the center of the can, but not above the small base of the tilted can. When you added water, the center of mass moved downward within the can (because of the extra mass of the water), adding stability. That new center was now above the base, so the can stayed up. So far, luckily, the Leaning Tower's center of mass has remained above its base. Now you know to expect trouble if those repairs haven't worked.

1 2 3 4 5 6 7 8 9 10 11 12 13 14 15 16 17 18 19 20 21 22 23 24 25 26 27 28 29 30
1 2 3 4 5 6 7 8 9 10 11 1

EXPERIMENT | 6

IT'S SINKING IN

Why aren't the world's biggest, most massive (heavy) buildings leaning, too? One good reason is that they're built on solid ground—*really* solid. New York's lofty sky-scrapers sit on tough granite that's billions of years old. Many of Europe's castles are built on hills, which tend to be made of the toughest rock that hasn't been worn down the way the stuff all around it has.

Meanwhile, the Leaning Tower of Pisa has a problem. The builders only dug down about 6 feet for its founda-tion, and that subsoil wasn't too solid—the big, heavy tower was built on soil that couldn't support it. Engineers have a word to describe a building's sinking into weak, uneven soil: subsidence. You can see its effects close-up in this experiment.

YOU WILL NEED

- ➤ **10 sheets of scrap paper**
- ➤ **Large dictionary (or telephone book)**
- ➤ **10 other books (preferably hardbacks)**
- ➤ **2 empty egg cartons (dozen-size)**

TAKE CARE!

It's best to do this one on a patio or other hard outdoor surface so you don't break anything inside.

1 Scrunch up enough scrap paper (into balls) to cover a 1-foot-square area on a hard floor (wood, tile, or concrete).

2 Starting with the dictionary, pile books on carefully, keeping the heaviest down low.

3 Continue until the books fall or the paper balls collapse, and count how many books you used.

4 Lay down the 2 empty egg cartons side by side on the paper balls and repeat Steps 2 and 3.

5 Repeat Steps 2 and 3 again, but lay the books down directly on the floor.

WHAT'S UP?

You've seen how your book "tower" stands up—literally—to different subsoils, or in this case paper, egg cartons, and a hard floor. If you can imagine Manhattan or the Scottish Highlands having a solid rock base like your floor, then you can see how tall buildings can be supported without swaying or tilting. Poor Pisa has a loose base that matches that scrunched-up paper. However, it's not quite the same all over that Cathedral Square. Remember that the two other, even larger, buildings next door are secure. The bell tower builders just ran out of luck—or solid stone to build on. And that's when the subsidence took over.

CHAPTER 4

THE COLLAPSING CATHEDRAL

"**W**e will construct a spire so high that once it's finished, those who see it will think that we were crazy!"

That doesn't exactly sound like a levelheaded engineer describing plans for a new project. In fact, the quote could probably be filed under "pipe dream" rather than something more practical-sounding . . . like "pipe works" or "drainpipes."

But those words announced the launch of a project to build the massive spire of Beauvais Cathedral, back in the mid-1500s. People *did* think the builders were crazy, because the spire came crashing down. The craziest thing is that the cathedral already had a 300-year-old track record for soaring structures that fell!

What drove the people of Beauvais to keep building up, only to see things come tumbling down? Was it something in the water? The local stinky cheese?

WHAT WENT WRONG?

IT ALL BEGAN IN 1225 when Bishop Milon de Nanteuil chose to build a new cathedral to replace an older, littler one at Beauvais, a small, prosperous city about 35 miles north of Paris. Ten years earlier, just across the Channel, a group of English noblemen had forced King John to sign the Magna Carta. That document limited the king's powers and forced him to recognize the rights of the nobles. The powerful French noblemen of northern France were also eager to demonstrate their importance. What better way than to help build a church that would be taller than any in France—even in Paris? It would certainly send a message to the French king.

The builders knew that the new cathedral would be massive, and parts of the foundation would extend more than 30 feet underground. But the main direction was up—the ceiling of the choir, just under 160 feet, would be the highest of any Christian church. Construction of the record-breaking choir was completed by 1272, but by 1284, parts of it had come tumbling down, so more pillars were added as an emergency measure. Then came

REACHING FOR HEAVEN

Beauvais Cathedral wasn't just intended to be big; its tall design was meant to symbolize man's reaching for heaven. The cathedral was also one of the finest—and most extreme—examples of Gothic architecture. Gothic churches used flying buttresses to support the weight of their walls. And that meant that walls could be thinner and higher, and could even have huge holes cut out of them for bright, colorful stained-glass windows.

FRANCE

the Hundred Years' War, so work on the nave (the main body of the cathedral) was put on hold.

Work resumed in 1500, concentrating on the transept (the bit that goes across the front of the nave, making the cross shape of a cathedral). When that was finished in 1548, the authorities decided to build a gigantic spire rather than set to work on the nave. That huge spire was completed in 1569. At 502 feet, it made Beauvais Cathedral the tallest building in the world. That record only lasted four years, though. On April 30, 1573, the spire and three levels of the bell tower came crashing down. Luckily, no one was badly hurt.

By now the cathedral organizers had run out of money—or maybe they'd run out of confidence that the cathedral would ever be finished. After a brief attempt to begin work on the nave in 1600, they called it a day. Beauvais Cathedral is still unfinished.

TURN BACK THE CLOCK

ONE MARK OF A good engineer or designer is being able to learn from the past. And the evidence suggests that the designers of Beauvais Cathedral knew their stuff—at least in most areas. Take the foundations, for instance: The Beauvais engineers were familiar with the triumphs of the past (like Notre Dame Cathedral, just down the road in Paris) as well as some of history's biggest no-nos, such as Fidenae Stadium and the Leaning Tower of Pisa.

They knew that their new cathedral was going to be massive, with enormous force pushing down into the surrounding soil. That would explain why parts of the cathedral are supported by foundations going more than 30 feet underground. They also knew that the flying buttresses—the go-to building feature for any Gothic architect—would transfer a lot of the force from the walls.

Gothic architecture was all about height and light, and the key to both were the flying buttresses. By channeling off lots of the lateral (horizontal) force of the building, the buttresses did part of the work that the walls normally did. That meant the walls could be thinner and even have spaces cut out for those lovely windows.

So far, so good. But the problems began when they started reaching for the sky. A taller building meant taller walls. Taller walls meant taller buttresses. But even buttresses have weight, so the designers made them thinner, and they became far less effective—particularly in the strong winds of northern France. Bad move.

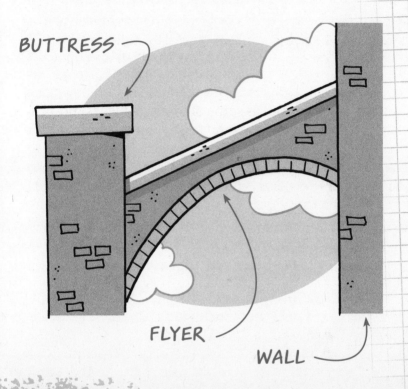

BUTTRESS

FLYER

WALL

FLYING BUTTRESSES

A buttress is any sort of building support that guards against the lateral (outward-pointing) forces on the walls by redirecting them to the ground. It works a bit like training wheels on a bike. A buttress can be solid, jutting out like a huge fin, but Gothic designers realized that they could still transfer the force across and down even if the buttress was only connected to the wall by a small arch called the "flyer."

FLYING HIGH

Now you know about the importance of buttresses—especially the flying variety—to Gothic buildings such as Beauvais Cathedral. And you know how those buttresses channel the lateral forces from the walls downward, so the walls stay upright. It's one thing knowing about these things on paper, but it's another to feel those forces for yourself. Here's a hands-on demonstration (literally) to help you "get the feel" of those forces in action.

YOU WILL NEED

- **4 friends**
- **Room with a slippery floor**

METHOD

1 Have 2 friends stand facing each other, wearing socks but not shoes.

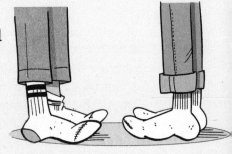

2 Ask those friends to take one pace back.

3 Now ask each of the other friends to sit on the floor behind the first pair, so that their backs are touching the back of the first pair's legs. (The second pair can still wear shoes.)

4 Ask the first pair to keep their feet in place and to hold their arms up.

5 Now ask them to lean forward so that their hands meet, forming an arch.

6 Ask the sitting pair whether they can feel the force pushing out from the arch.

WHAT'S UP?

Your friends have demonstrated—and experienced— what buttresses do when they capture lateral forces and redirect them downward. Flying buttresses do exactly that, even if they hardly seem to touch the walls they're supporting. And if one of your friends on the floor got up suddenly (like what might have happened when the wind blew a flyer off a Beauvais buttress), you can imagine what would happen. . . .

CHAPTER 5

THE TAY BRIDGE DISASTER

The British Empire was nearing the height of its power in the mid-19th century. While the British had already lost the Thirteen Colonies that became the United States, they still had control over huge parts of the world. In fact, it was said that "the sun never sets on the British Empire" because it would already be sunrise in Australia when it was still setting in Canada.

Driving this enormous empire was an island country, Great Britain, that had grown powerful through industry and engineering. And nowhere was that pride more evident than in Scotland, where steel mills, textile factories, and massive shipbuilding centers were the engines of wealth in the north of the island.

So it seemed fitting that an engineering marvel—the world's longest bridge—should connect one of Scotland's fastest-growing cities, Dundee, with the rest of the country. But this pride turned to horror one stormy night in 1879 when the Tay Bridge buckled and collapsed, taking an express train with it into the churning waters below.

WHAT WENT WRONG?

THE AGE OF THE railroad began in the early 19th century in Great Britain. By the 1870s, thousands of miles of train track connected once-remote parts of the world. The British constructed lines across the jungles, deserts, and mountains of their huge empire, and exported locomotives and rail equipment to many other countries.

Scotland was one of the main powerhouses of British industry, and railroad companies competed to build lines connecting Scottish cities with other British cities. One of Scotland's most important cities was fast-growing Dundee, which lies on Britain's east coast, on the northern bank of the River Tay. With Scottish engineering pride running high, it was decided to build a railroad bridge across the river to Edinburgh, the capital city.

From the start, people knew that this would become the world's longest bridge, and the noted engineer Sir Thomas Bouch had the job of designing it. In 1871, the work began. The

> **LATTICE GIRDER**
>
> An arrangement of metal beams, or girders, that are crisscrossed (latticed) to provide more strength.

bridge would consist of lattice girders held up by 90-foot-high towers, called piers. Bouch's original plan called for these piers to be sunk into bedrock beneath the river, but once work began, it became clear that the layer of bedrock was too far down. Instead, the piers rested on caissons, containers sunk into the riverbed and filled with concrete.

With the epically big Tay Bridge, Scotland had produced yet another engineering marvel. But everything was to change suddenly on the night of December 28, 1879. A storm had been raging all day, and witnesses recalled hurricane-force gusts cutting across the 250-foot span of the bridge, 100 feet above the cold water. Just after 7 p.m., the train from Edinburgh began crossing the bridge.

A ship's watchman on the river below saw the lights of the train as it approached the central spans, then a sudden gust of wind made him shield his eyes and blink. When he looked up again a moment later, the bridge was dark—there was no sign of the train. The entire central section of the Tay Bridge had collapsed, and the train had plunged 100 feet down into the river.

BEDROCK

A layer of strong solid rock, such as granite, that provides a secure base for buildings.

TURN BACK THE CLOCK

JUST WHAT DID cause the Tay Bridge to collapse so spectacularly? At first, it was hard to decide whether the design of the bridge itself was faulty or whether the problem was with the way the work had been carried out. The one known factor, of course, was the strong wind.

Four months before it opened to traffic in June 1878, a safety inspector observed the bridge and warned that the high winds might later cause problems. It turned out he was exactly right. To figure out how the wind caused the accident, think of a chair resting on a nonslip surface like a carpet. If you hold the back of the chair and push, the legs nearest you rise up. If those legs were attached to the floor, they'd be facing a force called tension, which would still be trying to lift them. The other legs would be pushed *down* with an opposite force called compression. The effect of wind pushing across a structure—like your push on the chair—is called wind loading.

Bouch had taken advice on wind loading from leading British engineers while designing the bridge. They advised him to prepare the bridge to withstand only 10 pounds per square inch (psi) of wind loading. At the same time, the builders of the Brooklyn Bridge were preparing for 50 psi, and the Eiffel Tower rating was even higher,

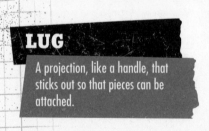

LUG
A projection, like a handle, that sticks out so that pieces can be attached.

at 55 psi. Modern skyscrapers are rated at 3,000 psi or even higher. So the design of this tall, narrow bridge definitely made it "underpowered" to deal with the wind.

Sure, Bouch got some crummy advice, but he comes under fire too, based on recent studies by a team of British scientists, who used a digital microscope to examine 135-year-old photographs of the Tay Bridge's remains. Dr. Peter Lewis concluded that Bouch made a bad choice when he selected the metal for the cross-bracing (another term for the lattice-girder arrangement) and lugs because its brittleness caused it to weaken—a clear case of "metal fatigue" (when metal gets weak from long or repeated stress). Although engineers at the time hadn't yet learned that concept, most knew enough to avoid using metals that suffered from it.

WIND LOAD

"I'll huff and I'll puff . . ."

The Scots are proud of their long history as inventors, especially in the field of engineering. But on that fateful night in 1879, an engineering marvel fell victim to the legendary Scottish wind. This experiment shows you how strong that unseen force of wind can be—and the part it played in sending a train into the icy waters below. The Tay Bridge had lattice girders like those in this experiment—you can see how they help maintain support.

YOU WILL NEED

- ➤ **3 pieces of wood of the same size (about 6 inches x 4 inches x 1 inch)**
- ➤ **Hair dryer**
- ➤ **Ruler**
- ➤ **Glue**
- ➤ **4 old nail files or Popsicle sticks (the longer the better)**

METHOD

1 Set up the 3 pieces of wood to make a basic bridge shape—2 of them standing upright a few inches apart and the third going across the top of them.

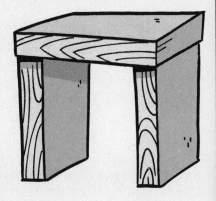

2 Try aiming the hair dryer at it at full blast. The bridge might topple. If it still stands, just poke it slightly with a ruler (remembering just how hard you tapped).

3 Set the "bridge" up again.

4 Glue two nail files diagonally from the left of the horizontal wood to midway down the right vertical piece of wood. Keep them close to each other.

5 Do the same from top right to middle left; the four sticks should form an *X*.

6 Wait for the glue to dry and repeat Step 2. The reinforced "bridge" should stay upright even after you've matched your previous force (from the hair dryer or tapping).

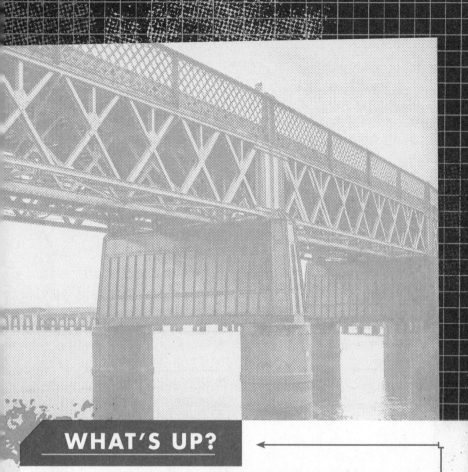

WHAT'S UP?

The crossed girders squeeze together when a lateral (horizontal) force acts on them, adding support to the structure. The Tay Bridge design did call for cross-bracing with its lattice girders. But as we know, it wasn't strong enough to withstand the powerful strain from wind loading on that December evening. Part of the reason *why* it wasn't strong enough crops up in the next experiment.

SNAP, CRACKLE ...

Engineering in action depends on how designs are put into practice—literally, getting down to nuts and bolts. When modern photography experts enlarged some of the images of the Tay Bridge disaster, they noticed that a lot of the problems could be traced to the lugs. These pieces of metal were crucial to every junction and held the cross-bracing together, and it seems that lots of them just "popped." This caused a chain reaction with the ones next to them popping—and eventually the whole bridge came apart as if someone had suddenly unzipped it.

This is probably the quickest, easiest experiment in the whole book, but it sheds light on one of the most devastating disasters in engineering history.

YOU WILL NEED

- ➤ **Gloves**
- ➤ **Paper clip**

METHOD

1 Put on a pair of gloves—just to be on the safe side (things could get a little hot).

2 Undo the paper clip and straighten it out.

3 Hold it as if you were pinching each end.

4 Bend it down so that the ends almost touch.

5 Bend it back so that it almost touches the other way.

6 Keep going back and forth repeatedly . . . until it snaps!

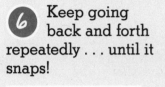

WHAT'S UP?

You've just demonstrated an engineering principle that every designer now takes into account but which wasn't yet studied back in the 1870s: metal fatigue. The metal weakens and often breaks after it has been put under prolonged or repeated stress—which is what you were doing by bending the paper clip back and forth. And all those lugs on the Tay Bridge were put under severe stress by the gale that night in 1879.

CHAPTER 6

THE "UNSINKABLE" TITANIC

On April 10, 1912, the British passenger liner *Titanic* set sail on its maiden voyage across the Atlantic. The ship was the largest and most famous in the world. Newspapers and magazines published photographs of its luxurious cabins, gymnasium, swimming pool, and the elegant grand staircase for first-class passengers. To top it all, the ship's owners claimed that its design made the *Titanic* "practically unsinkable."

Four days after setting sail, around midnight, the *Titanic* struck an iceberg. It soon became clear that the ship would not survive. Passengers crowded into lifeboats as the ship tilted more and more into the cold Atlantic water. Less than three hours after the collision, the *Titanic* broke apart and plunged to the bottom of the sea. More than 1,500 people died in one of the most dramatic shipping tragedies in history. The "practically unsinkable" ship had sunk.

WHAT WENT WRONG?

SHIPS AT THE TIME had no radar, Internet connection, or satellite navigation—the sort of crucial technology that help modern ships avoid the dangers of colliding with other ships and icebergs. Captain Edward Smith and his 885 crew members had to rely on their own eyesight and the telegraph reports from other ships nearby to spot danger.

At 11:40 p.m. on April 14, that danger arrived. The *Titanic* was traveling at 21 knots (24 mph), about 400 miles southeast of Newfoundland, Canada. An iceberg was spotted about a quarter of a mile ahead of the ship. It was too late to avoid it, though, and the iceberg side-swiped the ship's bow. It gouged out a number of slits along the starboard (right) edge of the *Titanic*.

Water rushed into six of the 16 watertight compartments, causing the ship to begin a slow dip forward, like a submarine preparing to dive. Alarms sounded, and at 12:40 a.m., passengers began boarding the lifeboats. Those familiar cries of "Women and children first!" rang out along the upper deck, which was tilting down deeper into the sea.

SISTER SHIPS

The *Titanic* was one of three liners built to almost identical designs by the White Star Line. The *Olympic* was launched in 1911. Its maiden voyage to New York went without a hitch, and the ship remained in service until 1935. The third ship, *Britannic*, was launched in 1914 and became a British hospital ship during World War I, until it struck a mine and sank in 1916. Violet Jessop, a nurse who survived the sinking of the *Britannic*, had also been on the *Titanic*'s ill-fated voyage.

Below deck, water was rushing into the compartments, adding weight and pulling the bow of the ship farther down. Passengers without first-class tickets had cabins in the lower decks. Many of them found doorways and staircases blocked—they would soon be going down with the ship.

All this time the *Titanic* was sending out distress calls by telegraph and shooting flares to attract the attention of any nearby ships, but to no avail. The ship continued to tilt downward until, at 2:20 a.m., it broke apart and sank. The passenger liner *Carpathia* arrived at the scene at 4 a.m. and took on board 710 survivors. Rough seas, thunderstorms, and more icebergs slowed the journey to New York, the doomed ship's original destination. A crowd of 40,000 people greeted the survivors nearly four days after the disaster.

TURN BACK THE CLOCK

MANY OF THE DESIGN decisions made about the *Titanic* were based on some basic engineering mistakes. The ship's designers divided the vessel into 16 "watertight" compartments, with vertical walls called bulkheads dividing them. If the ship collided with an object, the hull would be pierced and water would flow into one of the compartments. Doors on the bulkhead would close, so the watery compartment would resemble a dam. The designers pointed out that the ship could stay afloat with up to four compartments filled—but that's all.

All of this meant, in the owners' view, that the *Titanic* could hold out for days after a collision—easily enough time to reach a port safely. The owners were so confident in their "watertight compartment" design that they even considered reducing the small number of lifeboats because they spoiled the view for the first-class passengers! In fact, the ship's 20 lifeboats could only save 1,178 people, even though the *Titanic* had 2,223 people on board—something that's illegal these days.

BULKHEADS

Before you consider what could have been done to prevent the *Titanic* sinking, think about how it could ever have been expected to float in the first place. After all, this was a ginormous steel ship: 882 feet long, 175 feet high, and weighing more than 46,000 tons (that's right, *tons*). It floated because it followed the basic principle of buoyancy. Watertight compartments would keep the ship's density low and maintain its buoyancy. But if water overflowed from one compartment into its neighbor, then a lot of air would be driven out, making the ship sink faster.

That's exactly what happened on the *Titanic*. The bulkheads didn't go high enough, and water spilled over from one compartment to the next. Six compartments filled up with water—and the limit set by the engineering design was four. So instead of limping to a port, slightly wounded, the ship was doomed to sink.

BUOYANCY BASICS

If any object has a lower density than a liquid, then it floats. Density means, roughly, how much something weighs compared to how much space it takes up. The *Titanic* weighed a lot, but it was huge, and a lot of its size was taken up with air (in cabins, ballrooms, hallways, and other open areas). When it began taking on water, however, it became less buoyant and sank.

STAYING AFLOAT

Engineers love making models to test their ideas and to put them into practice on a small scale. In this simple experiment, you'll use your kitchen sink to stand in for the Atlantic Ocean. The goal is to see how buoyancy works in practice. The same principles that work to keep huge ships afloat also explain how you can keep your own miniboat from reaching SpongeBob's house on the ocean floor.

YOU WILL NEED

- Sink
- Water
- Modeling clay (or play dough)
- Paper towel

METHOD

1. Fill the plugged sink with water, almost to the very top.

2. Take a chunk of clay and roll it into a ball (about the size of a lemon).

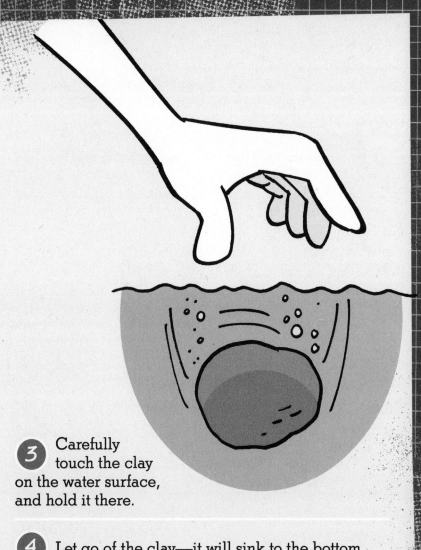

3 Carefully touch the clay on the water surface, and hold it there.

4 Let go of the clay—it will sink to the bottom.

5 Dry the clay with the paper towel and work it into the shape of a flat-bottomed boat (about the size of your palm). Make sure it has short sides pointing up.

CONTINUED

6 Carefully rest the boat on the water surface—this time it should float.

WHAT'S UP?

This experiment is an ideal demonstration of buoyancy at work. Buoyancy is really about the force of a liquid (the water in the sink here, or the Atlantic Ocean in the case of the *Titanic*) pushing up. Against it is the downward force of the object (the clay, or the *Titanic*), causing it to displace, or push away, water. When you get into the bathtub and it overflows, for instance, you've just displaced water.

If an object weighs less than the amount of water it displaces, it will float. The clay boat and the *Titanic* displaced a lot of water compared to their own weight, so they floated. The clay ball weighed the same, but its smaller, more compact size meant that it didn't displace much water—so it sank. And the *Titanic*, once it started taking on water (and weighing more), also sank.

OVERFLOW!

Once again you're approaching a problem like a real engineer—making a model to test a basic principle. This second experiment is also easy to do, but it goes right to the heart of the important engineering problems that led to the sinking of the *Titanic*.

The empty cubes in the plastic tray are standing in for the compartments on the *Titanic*. These were meant to be the engineering features that would make the ship "practically unsinkable." It was when water from some of those compartments spilled over into others that the real problems began—and disaster became inevitable.

YOU WILL NEED

> **Bathtub or sink**
> **Water**
> **Pitcher or plastic bottle**
> **Plastic ice cube tray**
> **Modeling clay or play dough (if needed)**

METHOD

1 Fill a plugged bathtub or sink more than halfway with water.

2 Fill the pitcher or bottle with water.

3 Place the ice cube tray on the surface of the water in the filled sink or tub, imagining the tray to be the *Titanic* and the cube shapes the compartments.

CONTINUED

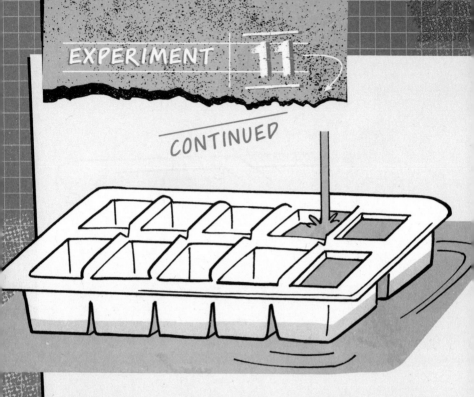

4 Carefully pour water from the pitcher into the two front-right "compartments." Check whether the tray floats.

5 Keep adding water to the second compartment and watch it overflow into the third.

6 Slowly keep filling the third, watching it overflow, and then the fourth compartment.

7 Continue until the ice cube tray tilts down and sinks.

8 Optional: Some ice cube trays are so buoyant that they won't sink on their own. If your tray doesn't sink, roll up marble-size balls of clay and add one to each compartment.

WHAT'S UP?

The designers of the *Titanic* had predicted that the ship would stay afloat even if four of its compartments were full of water. But on that April night, six of the *Titanic* compartments were damaged, and the water from some flowed into the others because the bulkheads weren't sealed at the top (as they are on modern ships). This experiment demonstrates how that happened, and how the bow (front) of the ship was dragged down by the weight of all the water filling those compartments.

CHAPTER 7

THE BOSTON MOLASSES FLOOD

"**H**eard the one about the killer Molasses Flood?" "Oh, sure. Wasn't that around the same time as the terrible ice-cream glacier—or was it the cotton-candy eruption?"

That would be most people's reaction to the news that the city of Boston suffered a terrible molasses flood in 1919. But it's true, and as the saying goes, "Truth is stranger than fiction." As you get your head around the fact that 2.3 million gallons of molasses might have been stored in a 50-foot-high tank, which burst open to cause the flood, you come across some really scary facts. For one thing, the molasses traveled at 35 miles per hour, meaning that anyone or anything in its path—people, horses, buses—had no chance to escape. In fact, 21 people died and 150 were injured.

People said that decades later you could smell the remains of the molasses on hot summer days. That may or may not be true, but it still leaves the big question: Just how did this flood occur, and did the molasses really flow that fast—in the cold of January?

WHAT WENT WRONG?

IT WAS JUST AFTER noon on a Wednesday in Boston, and people were feeling pretty happy. World War I had ended two months earlier, and the Red Sox (led by a young Babe Ruth) had recently won their second World Series in three years. To top things off, the relatively mild weather promised a hint of spring.

People in the North End, an industrial area not far from downtown, were going about their business. Some workmen even felt it was warm enough to have their lunch outside, in the shadow of the U.S. Industrial Alcohol molasses tank. The tank, made of curved sheet metal, rose 50 feet up from street level and was jampacked with crude molasses (sugar in liquid form).

At 12:40 p.m., people began to hear a low rumbling sound from the tank. Before anyone had time to guess what it was, a wall of molasses 8 to 25 feet high came rushing from the tank and down the streets. It traveled at an astonishing 35 miles per hour—faster than any vehicles on Boston's streets at the time.

The Boston *Evening Globe* described the scene: "Fragments of the great tank were thrown into the air,

THE TRIANGULAR TRADE

What was all that molasses doing in Boston, anyway? The story goes back centuries to Colonial times, when molasses from the Caribbean islands would be shipped to Boston to be turned into rum. Some of that rum would be shipped for sale in West Africa, where the American merchants would use the money to buy slaves to be sent to the Caribbean . . . where they would pick more sugarcane to turn into molasses. By 1919, though, slavery was abolished and the molasses was more likely to be used to make industrial alcohol than rum.

buildings in the neighborhood began to crumple up as though the underpinnings had been pulled away from under them, and scores of people in the various buildings were buried in the ruins, some dead and others badly injured."

Those who witnessed the flood—which some have compared to a tsunami—couldn't believe their eyes. Fallen elevated train tracks, crumpled buildings, and overturned vehicles mingled in the gooey mess once the wave had passed. Medical teams arrived and had to wade waist-deep through molasses to reach some of the injured. The cleanup operation took months, using huge amounts of salt water and sand to wash away or soak up the molasses.

TURN BACK THE CLOCK

ENGINEERS AT THE time agreed that the tank exploded because of structural defects combined with unseasonably warm temperatures. But when victims and their families took the U.S. Industrial Alcohol Company to court, the molasses company was quick to pass the blame, claiming political extremists had bombed the tank.

One of the lawsuits against the company was filed by the Boston Elevated Train line, which had lost an elevated track in the disaster. This company hired one of the most respected engineers in the country, Professor Charles Spofford, to prove that the tank owners were at fault. Spofford took pieces of the tank back to his lab at Massachusetts Institute of Technology, just a few miles away in Cambridge.

After careful examination and tests, Spofford concluded that the plates were too thin to withstand the pressure of all the molasses inside. Plus, the tank had far too few rivets to join the pieces of metal securely, so the rivets would have popped out. Witness statements support this view: People reported rivets shooting out everywhere "like machine gun bullets."

The bomb theory had been disproved, and it was apparent that the problem was in the tank's design. Investigators examined the construction of the tank and found even more alarming evidence. The man who oversaw the building of the tank in 1915 was neither an architect nor an engineer—it turns out he couldn't even read a blueprint! Local residents pointed out that the tank had leaked from day one. Rather than fix the problem, the owners simply painted the tank brown so no one would notice.

WHEN IS A LIQUID NOT A LIQUID?

One puzzling feature of the molasses flood is its speed. Molasses is an interesting substance that scientists call a non-Newtonian fluid. The high viscosity ("goopiness") of these fluids, including ketchup, toothpaste, and whipped cream, changes when forces act on them. That's why ketchup might seem to take forever to come out of the bottle—until you give the bottle a sharp tap. The molasses in the tank was under a lot of pressure, so when the tank burst, it came shooting out.

HOLDING UP TO PRESSURE

The expert analysis of the molasses tank fragments showed that the metal was too weak—with too few rivets—to withstand the pressure of the molasses inside. Part of the pressure, people believe, was caused by gas produced as the molasses fermented (that's when some of the sugar begins turning to alcohol, producing gas as a by-product).

But simply having so much liquid (more than 2 million gallons) inside the tank was the biggest reason it burst. The depth of the liquid—about 50 feet—added pressure, especially near the bottom of the tank. You get the same sense of pressure the deeper you swim underwater.

This demonstration lets you see how that pressure increases with depth. Plus, you can get an idea of what that pressure does to a liquid when it gives it a chance to escape.

YOU WILL NEED

- **3 empty large plastic soda bottles (it's important they're the same size)**
- **Sharp pencil or pointed knife**
- **2 friends**
- **Water**

TAKE CARE!

Things could get a little wet, so you'd better do this one outside! And always be extra careful when using a sharp pencil or knife.

METHOD

1 Use the pencil or knife to poke a hole about the width of the pencil in the first bottle, about 2 inches down from the top.

2 Repeat Step 1 for the second bottle, poking the hole about midway down.

3 Repeat Step 1 for the third bottle, poking the hole about an inch from the bottom.

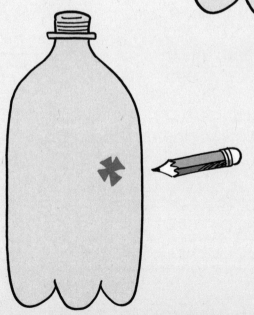

CONTINUED

4 Give a bottle to each friend, keeping one for yourself. Each of you will plug the hole of your bottle with your finger and fill the bottle to the top with water.

5 Line up the bottles 2 feet apart, with their holes pointing away. Get your friends to pull their fingers away and note how far each stream of water shoots.

6 Compare the length of each trail of water.

WHAT'S UP?

You can see how the pressure of the extra depth exerted a greater force on the water so that the water shot out farther. That's why the bottle with the hole closest to its base probably shot out water the farthest. Imagine the pressure exerted at the base of the 2.3-million-gallon molasses tank!

SLOW AS MOLASSES?

Here's a way to imagine the sort of shock Bostonians must have had as the molasses tank gave way in January 1919. It was really a double shock—first that the tank had burst, and then that its contents were racing out so quickly.

We now know that molasses, as a non-Newtonian fluid, does behave differently according to the pressure applied to it. This experiment is really a fun demonstration of a sudden force—you—acting on another non-Newtonian fluid—toothpaste.

YOU WILL NEED

➤ **Tube of the cheapest toothpaste you can find**

METHOD

1 Make sure you're outside for this demonstration.

2 Take the cap off the toothpaste and lay it on the ground. Note that nothing flows out.

3 Press a finger lightly down on the tube for a second and note how some of the toothpaste flows out slowly.

4 Make sure there's no one "in the firing line," raise your leg over the toothpaste, and stamp down on it as hard as you can.

WHAT'S UP?

You've just applied a sudden force to a non-Newtonian fluid . . . in the interest of science, of course. Non-Newtonian fluids act differently, depending on how much force you apply to them. With no extra pressure, the fluid remained stationary in the tube, and then only flowed slowly when the small force of your finger was applied to it. But with the sudden and large force of your stomp, it flowed out at high speed, just like the contents of that tank in Boston.

CHAPTER 8

THE HINDENBURG CRASHES

The last, tragic moments of the German airship *Hindenburg*, engulfed in flames and falling to earth, were captured on film and described live by an emotional radio announcer. Millions heard his tearful voice crying out, "Oh, the humanity!" These days we have become accustomed to seeing dramatic events unfold in real time, but in the 1930s, the experience was new and unsettling. The entire world had become a witness to the disaster at Lakehurst Naval Air Station in New Jersey.

Mystery still surrounds the reason for the crash, and that uncertainty set the airship industry back by decades. Will airships ever make their return in big numbers? That might only happen when we work out the real reason for this fiery crash.

WHAT WENT WRONG?

BACK IN THE EARLY 1930s, most people wishing to cross the Atlantic had to travel by ship, a trip that took about a week. Commercial air travel existed, but planes just weren't big or powerful enough to carry the extra fuel that passengers and their baggage would require for such a long journey. Plus, most of those passenger planes were cramped and uncomfortable—even compared to today's economy seats!

In 1930, Germany provided an alternative that combined the comfort and luxury of ocean liners with the speed of air travel. Passenger services began that year on airships, huge cigar-shaped inflatable balloons with engines and cabins attached. These airships were sometimes called zeppelins, after the German Count Ferdinand von Zeppelin, who designed the first one in 1895. Zeppelins had appeared in the skies before, as bombers during World War I. When Adolf Hitler and his Nazi Party took control of Germany in 1933, the new zeppelins were a symbol of national pride and engineering power.

In 1936, Germany launched the LZ 129 *Hindenburg*. At more than 800 feet long and 130 feet wide, it was the largest aircraft ever to fly. As many as 50 crew members piloted the craft and saw to the needs of up to 72 passengers on each crossing from Germany to a special landing field at Lakehurst Naval Air Station in New Jersey.

After almost 20 successful round-trips across the Atlantic Ocean, the last journey began in Frankfurt, Germany, on May 4,

1937. Two days later, the *Hindenburg* passed majestically over New York City and approached its landing field in New Jersey. It was delayed for about an hour by thunderstorms and hovered in the area until conditions improved. With the *Hindenburg* about 200 feet up, the captain finally ordered mooring ropes to be lowered so the ground crew could guide the airship down safely.

Then witnesses on the ground saw a blue glow on top of the *Hindenburg,* followed by flames near its tail. A split-second later, a huge explosion turned the airship into a fireball. Still burning ferociously, the zeppelin began to break up and settle to earth. The *Hindenburg* had been destroyed, along with—it seemed—the future of airships.

TURN BACK THE CLOCK

THE *HINDENBURG* crash is as much a mystery story as it is an engineering and design failure. With World War II drawing near, had people with anti-Nazi views sabotaged the mighty airship? That was certainly the conclusion of many proud Germans, who wouldn't accept that the airship might have been the victim of poor design or construction.

Sabotage, design, and construction lead to one word: hydrogen. The *Hindenburg* floated above the ground because its "envelope" (the cigar-shaped balloon) was filled with the gas hydrogen. Hydrogen is the lightest chemical element—much lighter than air—so it provided the necessary lift to make the ship fly. Hydrogen is also known for igniting quickly and easily. Airships using hydrogen needed protective measures to keep the gas away from open flames or sudden heat.

SABOTAGE

Destroying or damaging something deliberately, and usually secretly.

Most people agree that the *Hindenburg* crashed because its hydrogen ignited. The question of how is still a mystery that fills pages of books and the Internet. It's unlikely that the airship was sabotaged, because German officials had checked the details of the crew and passengers before the flight. Likewise, the U.S. military would have noticed any gunshot, bomb, or other attempts to ignite the hydrogen from someone on the ground.

Modern aircraft engineers have examined films of the *Hindenburg* crash to try to solve the mystery. One theory suggests that static electricity traveled 200 feet up the mooring cables and caused a spark that ignited the hydrogen. Another says that the electrical storms that evening caused a spark in the metal framework, which then set things off.

These days, airships are used for advertising, observation, and exploration, and some are once more being used for transportation. Not surprisingly, modern airships no longer use hydrogen: Their "lifting gas" is either helium or hot air (which uses the same principle as hot-air balloons). So the answer to the question "How could this disaster have been avoided?" is pretty simple: Skip the hydrogen next time!

WHY NOT HELIUM?

If hydrogen is so dangerous, why didn't the Germans fill the *Hindenburg*'s envelope with helium? After all, the party balloon—filling gas is almost as light as hydrogen and doesn't burn. Well, in the 1930s, helium was much rarer than hydrogen, and the United States was the only country that had much of it. Americans were in no rush to give any helium to the Germans, and Congress had recently passed the Helium Control Act of 1927, banning exports of the gas.

DON'T GIVE ME STATIC

One of the likeliest causes of the *Hindenburg* explosion was a buildup of static electricity caused by the electrical storms in the area. According to this theory, dropping the mooring cables grounded the airship, creating a flow of electrons and sparks, and it was one of those sparks that lit the hydrogen. But your demonstration can show how even a small amount of static electricity can pack a huge punch.

This awesome experiment works really well if you have a long stretch of smooth floor, like a school hallway (but you might want to steer clear of the principal's office). You can even turn the demonstration into a contest, to see who can pull their can the farthest.

YOU WILL NEED

- 1 to 3 friends
- 1 balloon per person
- 1 empty soda can per person
- Long straight hallway or other open stretch of smooth floor
- Wool cloth (optional)

METHOD

1 Each "player" should blow up a balloon and tie it. Each takes the next steps in turn.

2 Lay the soda can on the floor so that it could roll down the hall.

3 Rub the balloon vigorously against your hair (or wool cloth if your hair is too short).

4 Stand in front of the can, facing toward it, and lower the balloon.

5 The can will roll toward the balloon. That's when the person has to walk slowly backward, keeping the can rolling.

6 The person who rolls the can the farthest without letting it stop is the winner.

WHAT'S UP?

You're working with static electricity here, but luckily it's not going to produce a *Hindenburg*-style disaster. Rubbing the balloon against your hair causes electrons (negatively charged particles) to be rubbed off onto the balloon's surface. That gives the balloon a negative charge. The surface of the can is slightly positive, so the opposites attract. The positively charged can then follows the balloon until the can has attracted enough of the balloon's electrons to make the charges equal.

DOWN IN FLAMES

The key to the *Hindenburg* disaster was the way in which the hydrogen ignited so quickly, causing the explosion. One current theory about why this happened blames the type of paint on the outside of the envelope (balloon section). This paint contained chemicals to add strength to the envelope's shell, making it fly more securely.

The humongous problem was that this paint was extremely flammable—definitely a bad idea. Modern airships, even though they no longer use hydrogen as a lifting gas, must combine stability with being fireproof. You can run a quick test with this experiment to show how a very basic ingredient can be used to protect the shell of a balloon against flames.

This isn't a dangerous experiment, but the goggles and glove are a precaution in case things blow quickly and catch you off guard.

YOU WILL NEED

- ➤ **Matches**
- ➤ **Candle (ideally the sort that sits in a glass cup)**
- ➤ **2 or 3 party balloons**
- ➤ **Goggles**
- ➤ **Glove**
- ➤ **Measuring cup**
- ➤ **Water**
- ➤ **Friend**

CONTINUED

METHOD

1 Light the candle and leave it burning on top of a table.

2 Blow up a balloon and tie it shut.

3 Put on the goggles, then put a glove on one hand and hold the balloon with that hand.

4 Slowly and carefully lower the balloon down toward the burning candle. It should pop just above the candle.

5 Now fill the measuring cup with water and ask your friend to hold the mouth of another balloon open.

6 Pour as much water as you can into the balloon. This will probably amount to 2 to 3 tablespoons.

7 Blow up the balloon and tie it.

8 Repeats Steps 3 and 4. Hold the balloon over the candle for 5 seconds—it shouldn't burst.

WHAT'S UP?

You've just used one of the qualities of water to "treat" (using one substance to strengthen another) the shell of the balloon—it absorbs the heat of the flame rather than letting that heat burn a hole through the balloon's skin. Modern airship skins don't use water, but their fabric is treated with materials that either resist or absorb heat to prevent explosions.

CHAPTER 9

THE TACOMA NARROWS BRIDGE

Engineering students sometimes get to watch movies at the start of the school year to help them understand the principles of engineering and design—a fun way to get away from thick textbooks and long lectures. One clip gets even the most daydream-y student staring in disbelief at the screen. This "main attraction" shows a suspension bridge that looks a lot like the Golden Gate Bridge. A hat blows past the camera, so it's pretty obvious that it's windy. And those bulging cars with spare tires on the back must come from the 1930s, right?

Just when it looks like someone's dull home movie, something strange starts to happen. The roadway across the bridge starts to sway and kink, as if someone has flicked a giant jump rope. Up and down it swings, looking more like a ribbon than a combination of asphalt, concrete, and steel. There's even a car left on the bridge and—*whoa!* The road just tears in two and flops down like two rags.

What in the world was *that* all about? A tipsy cameraman? Trick photography? That's not how bridges are meant to behave!

WHAT WENT WRONG?

THE TACOMA NARROWS Bridge is a case study for anyone interested in civil engineering, road safety, bridges . . . or the just plain crazy behavior of inanimate objects. This suspension bridge, crossing Puget Sound in Washington State, was the third-longest bridge in the world, although it was only 39 feet wide. That long-narrow combination is a big clue as to why it met such a dramatic end. And it explains how a solid bridge might wind up behaving like a jump rope.

Leon Moisseiff was the engineer in charge of constructing the Tacoma Narrows Bridge. He changed some of the original plans to make the bridge narrower and lighter, and believed that the modified design would save money without affecting the strength of the bridge. One of the important features of Moisseiff's design was its lack of stiffening trusses. He wanted to produce a graceful bridge, and those and V-shaped supports under the road looked like ugly scaffolding or training wheels on a bike. That change meant that his new bridge would only be a third as stiff as similar bridges, such as San Francisco's Golden Gate Bridge and New York City's George Washington Bridge. Is that such a big deal? You bet. The Pacific Northwest is noted for its rain and fog, but it also has high winds. Just days after the Tacoma Narrows Bridge opened in July 1940, the roadway (or "deck") began to move up and down, even in a slight wind.

STIFFENING TRUSS

A V-shaped pair of girders (beams) linking the columns of a suspension-bridge tower to provide strength and stiffness.

Just after 7 a.m. on November 7, 1940, Kenneth Arkin, the chairman of the Washington State Toll Bridge Authority, arrived at the bridge after awakening to the sound of wind. Arkin found the bridge moving

The Tacoma Narrows Bridge began its movements while it was being constructed. Workers even complained of seasickness. Once the bridge opened and its reputation for moving grew, thrill-seekers began to arrive. They were attracted by the fairground excitement of seeing oncoming cars disappear and then reappear as the deck moved up and down in the wind. The bridge was soon nicknamed "Galloping Gertie" because of this movement.

more than three feet up and down about once every two seconds. At 10 o'clock, he halted all traffic. Within half an hour, the support cables in the center of the bridge began to snap, causing the deck to swing even more wildly. Then the deck broke apart, drawing the two main towers toward the center and completing the collapse. Fortunately no one was injured—but the results were catastrophic and it took 10 years to rebuild.

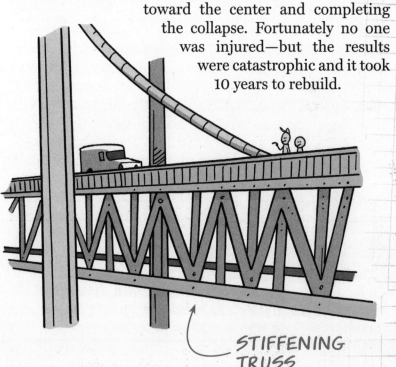

STIFFENING
TRUSS

TURN BACK THE CLOCK

AT THE HEART OF the Tacoma Narrows Bridge's collapse lies a puzzle. Can the lateral (side-to-side) forces of wind cause a structure to move up and down? Modern scientists certainly think so, and builders and engineers living before the Tacoma Narrows Bridge collapse had reported just such up-and-down movement caused by wind elsewhere. They observed which bridges did and didn't suffer from it and built accordingly, even if they couldn't provide a full scientific explanation.

Throughout the 19th century, engineers and the general public noted that suspension bridges did move up and down when wind blew across them. John Roebling's 1870 design for the Brooklyn Bridge, which opened in 1883, took those wind forces into account. And the stiffening trusses in the Golden Gate and other suspension bridges also reduced this effect.

The key to the puzzling collapse of the Tacoma Narrows Bridge was the switch from vertical (up and down) vibration to torsional (twisting) movements, which can severely weaken the materials in the roadway across a bridge. The curve of the vibrating bridge caused some of the wind to spiral. The spinning motion of these pockets of spiral wind then started to cause a twisting motion of the bridge (this is where engineers start filling blackboards with complicated equations, by the way). The

increased vibrations eventually caused a cable to snap,
turning the vibrations into
destructive twists. At that
point, the wind was hardly
needed, and the bridge
could stand no more.

The Tacoma design did
call for dampers to reduce
the vibrations and cable swing, but these proved to be
too weak. In the end, the vibrations grew strong enough
to break the cable connections. That made the deck
uneven, because one side then hung lower, and the up-
and-down motion became a twisting motion. It was the
twisting that did the damage, tearing apart the deck,
snapping even more cables, and causing the bridge to
collapse.

DAMPER

DAMPING TACTICS

Modern engineers, architects, and builders have learned a lot of lessons from the Tacoma Narrows Bridge collapse. In addition to running designs through all sorts of lab tests for wind, rain, earthquakes, and sudden temperature changes, they now remember to go back to basics.

The Tacoma Narrows Bridge did have dampers—simple but essential devices to absorb some of the vibrations of the cables and of the bridge itself—but these weren't up to the job and failed that fateful November morning. Just how do dampers work? Well, since you probably don't have a spare suspension bridge lying around in your bedroom, you'll just have to build your own damper.

YOU WILL NEED

- **2 empty 1-gallon plastic bottles (with handles)**
- **Water**
- **6-foot jump rope**
- **2 friends**
- **Playground swing**
- **Watch or timer**

METHOD

1. Fill both bottles with water and tighten the lids.

2. Feed one end of the jump rope through the handle of one of the bottles so there's an equal amount of rope on each side.

3. Have one friend sit on the swing, ready to go.

4 Pull back your friend on the swing until the swing is at the height of your shoulders.

5 Ask your other friend, the "timer," to get ready, then let go and ask the "swinger" to hold on and not move—just let the swing go back and forth.

6 Ask the timer how long it swung until she stopped, then let her get off the swing.

7 Now hold up the bottle with the rope next to the swing and feed the two handles of the rope through the brace on the seat. Have your timer hold the bottle.

8 Have your swinger hold up the other bottle while you feed one of the rope handles through the other brace of the swing and then through the handle of the other bottle.

9 Tie the ends of the rope together. You should now have two bottles tied together in a rope loop and hanging, one on each side of the swing.

10 Repeat Steps 3 to 6.

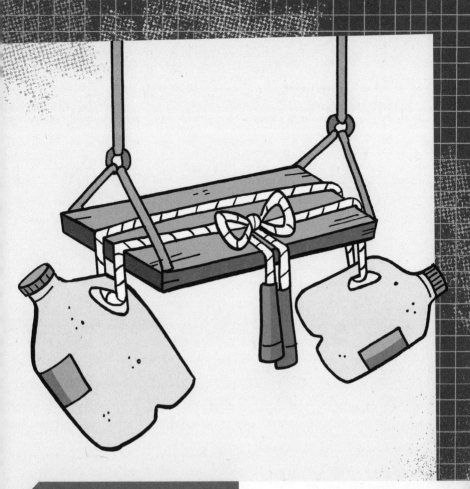

You've used the bottle arrangement to create a damper, just as engineers incorporate them into the designs of bridges, skyscrapers, and overpasses. The damper absorbs some of the force from the swing, lessening its movement. That's why it should take less time to come to a stop when you have the bottle arrangement in place.

CHAPTER 10

SHERMAN TANKS GET STUCK

Thousands of American soldiers were getting their first taste of war in Europe. They had been hunkered down by the French coast for a few days, engaged in some of the most brutal fighting of World War II. Now the time had come to fight their way even farther into France.

The Nazi war machine had been expecting a big invasion, even if the commanders weren't sure exactly where it would land in France. The Americans and their allies knew that a real fight lay ahead if they were to drive the Germans out of France altogether, but the Allies had two big advantages. One was air power, and planes kept pounding German positions whenever the skies cleared. Another was the Sherman tank, which had played a big part in Allied victories in the North African desert two years before.

Sherman tanks led the advance from the beaches and into the countryside. They plowed through hedges as if they were made of straw. But then . . . many of them got stuck, like cars with no snow tires in a blizzard. And a tank that's stuck is just a sitting duck. What was going on here?

WHAT WENT WRONG?

ON JUNE 6, 1944, the world witnessed the biggest seaborne invasion in history. More than 5,000 ships carrying 160,000 troops left England before dawn. Hours later they had arrived along a 50-mile stretch of coastline in northern France. Small vessels ferried the soldiers to shore, where they faced the full might of the German army. The Allied forces of the United States, Britain, and Canada eventually overturned the German shore defenses and gained a foothold on the European mainland. We remember that date as D-Day.

Getting to shore and surviving was only the start of the real fighting. German defenses stretched far inland, and the German army was determined to drive the Allies back to the sea. But more Allied soldiers began arriving, along with heavy equipment. One of the most eagerly awaited arrivals was the mighty Sherman tank.

The Allies planned to fan out from the beaches and fight their way eastward across France and Belgium and into Germany itself, but first they had to deal with the stubborn German opposition just ahead of them in France. Here was a chance for those Sherman tanks to blast their way through German lines—but many of them had hardly gone more than a mile before they got stuck in the soft, muddy soil.

Waiting for the Sherman tanks in northern France were two powerful German tanks—the Tiger and the Panther. Both were heavier than the Sherman, with

ON THE PLUS SIDE

The Sherman tank did have lots of advantages. It was medium size, which meant that lots of them could be transported easily on ships or trains. Plus, it could be made quickly in American automobile factories that now devoted themselves to the war effort. More than 50,000 Sherman tanks were produced on those assembly lines. And on hard ground—or along roads near battlefields—the Sherman was a nimble addition to American firepower.

armor that was twice as thick. They carried much more powerful guns, which were able to shoot farther and pierce enemy armor more effectively. One American tank commander described the German explosives as cutting through the Sherman armor "like a hot knife through butter." Although both of these German tanks were slower than the Sherman on firm ground, their wider tracks were much better suited to the soft soil of northern Europe.

TURN BACK THE CLOCK

MILITARY ENGINEERS today often refer to the Sherman tank when they examine ways to combine firepower and speed with armor protection for the tank crew. They have an advantage over the Sherman's designers, who needed to get lots of tanks produced quickly before they had much time to do test runs. In a way, the experience of the Shermans in World War II battle became a test run for future tank design.

Several of the Sherman's features were based on inaccurate ideas of battle conditions in Europe. Designers gave the tanks narrow tracks, a relatively light gun, and lightweight armor to help them travel quickly, but with so many Shermans getting stuck in the soft soil of France, these features only made the tanks more vulnerable to attack. The builders of the Sherman tanks were also told to produce an engine that would be powerful and yet still light. They modified an aircraft engine (which had both of those qualities), but its fuel was far more flammable than most tank fuels. It was common for a single

German shell not just to pierce the armor of a Sherman but to turn it into a fireball. It's obvious that a new tank design would have to overcome those problems. The Pershing tank, the Sherman's successor, managed to do so but arrived too late to play a part in World War II.

Even while the Shermans were involved with fighting, the Allies looked for ways to compete with the

German tanks. It was impossible to add a new layer of armor to the tanks in the field, but tank crews tried to add a little more protection. They gathered whatever they could find—bits of timber, sandbags, even chicken wire—to attach to the sides and fronts of the Shermans. It's hard to say how effective these measures were, but at least the crews felt that they had something more around them.

Another change was far more successful. Tank crews fitted special extensions, called duckbills, onto the sides of the Shermans' narrow tracks. These gave the Shermans better "footing" to match that of the German tanks, but the extensions fell off if the tank went too fast.

ELEPHANT'S FOOTPRINT

Although the Sherman weighed far less than the Tiger and Panther tanks, these German models had much wider tracks. That meant that the weight was spread out over a wider area and the tank didn't sink as much. If you've read about elephants' footprints, you'll know that the same principle applies. Those big, wide elephant feet spread the weight around so well that an elephant's footprint isn't even as deep as that of a high-heel shoe.

Scientists and engineers use the term "quick and dirty" to describe demonstrations and experiments that get the job done fast even if they're not conducted with a strict scientific process. Here's a good quick-and-dirty demonstration (literally) to help you get a handle on those poor tracks on the Sherman tanks.

YOU WILL NEED

> Glue
> Old pair of shoes
> 2 shoeboxes (preferably wider boxes that contained boots)
> Patch of loose soil waiting to be planted
> Rake
> Ordinary shoes
> Ruler

METHOD

1   Glue each of the old shoes to the inside bases of the shoeboxes.

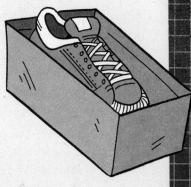

2   Find or prepare a patch of soil about 3 feet square. (It could be part of a garden waiting to be planted.)

3   Rake away any stones and twigs so the surface is even and smooth.

4 Wearing your normal shoes, step into the patch of soil and stand still, with both feet on the soil.

5 Step out again and use the ruler to measure how far down your footprint went.

6 Rake the soil smooth again.

7 The next bit might be awkward, but repeat Steps 4 and 5 wearing the glued shoes.

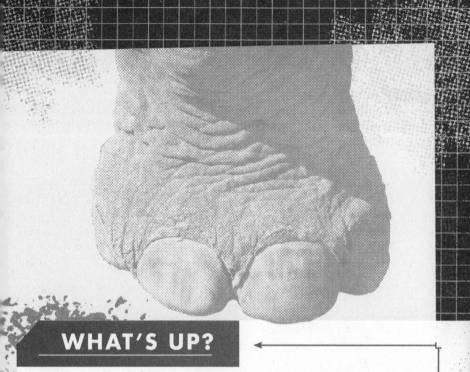

WHAT'S UP?

You've just demonstrated the principle behind the shallow elephant footprint—and the reason why Sherman tanks sank while the heavier German tanks didn't. You should've found that the depth of your footprint was smaller in the second test. It's all down to pressure.

Scientists measure Pressure (in this case, seen as the depth of the footprint) by dividing Force by Area. Written as an equation, that's $P = F / A$. During the experiment, the force (how much gravity draws you down) was the same both times but the area was different. Your shoes take up less area than a shoebox, so that means that the pressure is greater (the force is divided by a smaller number). The opposite is true—the pressure is less—when the force is divided by the bigger number (the larger area of the box). So a wider tank track, even if it's a little heavier, will sink less in soft soil.

CHAPTER 11

FLIGHT OF THE "SPRUCE GOOSE"

If ever there was a story of extremes, it's that of the H-4 Hercules aircraft, known as the "Spruce Goose." Where do we start? Well, it was bigger than any aircraft made before it, and it still holds the record for the widest wingspan. It took years to design and build. The plane was the brainchild of Howard Hughes, one of the world's most eccentric billionaires.

Despite delays, grumbling about taxpayers' money, and the enormous scale of the project, the plane was finally finished. Okay, it was more than two years after World War II ended, and the plane was meant to transport soldiers and tanks across the Atlantic Ocean. But on November 2, 1947, the Spruce Goose floated out onto a Californian harbor, revved up its engines, picked up speed, and left the ground. It climbed to a height of 70 feet, did a one-mile circuit over Long Beach harbor, and then landed.

That was it—the single flight of the Spruce Goose. Never again would it leave its climate-controlled hangar, at a jumbo-size cost to Hughes of $1 million a year (more than $10 million in today's dollars). Was it the most expensive toy ever made, or an example of the world not recognizing a genius at work?

WHAT WENT WRONG?

ONCE THE UNITED States entered World War II in late 1941, the military needed to send thousands of troops and thousands of tons of equipment across the Atlantic Ocean. But crossing the Atlantic was no easy matter: Ships were easy targets for German submarines, or U-boats, as they were called. Congress considered an alternative—building huge planes to fly men and materials to Europe in "flying boats" able to take off and land on water rather than on normal runways. And they'd need to carry a load of 35 tons—that's 70,000 pounds!

In October 1942, Congress turned to the Hughes Aircraft Corporation to produce such a plane. As the plans evolved, it was clear that the ambitious Hughes was working on a "scaled-up" eight-engine plane with more than double the cargo load first suggested. With a

FLYING BOATS

A flying boat can take off from and land on water. Unlike a float plane, which uses floats attached to the wings, a flying boat's fuselage (the main body of an aircraft) itself is buoyant. The wood construction of the Spruce Goose would have helped achieve that goal.

150,000-pound cargo capacity, the plane could carry up to 750 fully equipped troops or two 30-ton M4 Sherman tanks.

Hughes faced another big obstacle—materials. During the war, metals like steel and aluminum were in short supply, so the plane was made almost completely of birch plywood, but somehow the H-4 Hercules got nicknamed the "Spruce Goose." Why? Well, the construction workers imagined the plane taking off from the water like a giant wooden goose, and "Spruce Goose" had a nice ring to it.

SCALING UP

Increasing the size of something while keeping the same proportions.

By the time the war ended in 1945, the Spruce Goose was still unfinished and Hughes had become the target of criticism and mockery. He remained defiant that he had produced the right plane, though, and it was in that defiant mood that he invited journalists onto the plane on November 2, 1947. He wanted to show the plane's ability to taxi across the water with Hughes himself at the controls. The plane did two crossings of Long Beach harbor, but instead of guiding it back, Hughes revved the engines, turned, and took the Spruce Goose on its only flight. Was that flight a success or a failure? People still argue that question to this day.

TURN BACK THE CLOCK

DO WE REALLY need to turn back the clock to study the H-4 Hercules? Did it really fail? After all, it was eventually built to the design that Howard Hughes chose, even if that design changed a lot along the way. Plus, it really did fly— even if it was only for about a mile and for no more than a couple of minutes.

But these facts overlook something essential: The war had finished two years before that brief test flight, and the whole purpose of the plane was to transport troops and heavy equipment. There was no more need to fly hundreds of soldiers across thousands of miles. There's also the matter of the price tag—taxpayers must have felt a little cheated to see what $22 million of their money bought.

Ever since the 1947 test flight, critics have claimed that the Spruce Goose couldn't have climbed beyond the 70 feet that it reached. They say that a condition known as "ground effect" kept the plane airborne at that level: Near the ground, an aircraft gets more lift (to help flight) and has less drag (to slow it down). But in 2014, flight

THE MYSTERIOUS MILLIONAIRE

Howard Hughes was born in 1905, the son of a wealthy inventor and businessman. As a young man, Hughes used some of his fortune to produce films in Hollywood, but his real love was flying. In 1932, he founded the Hughes Aircraft Company and began designing and testing high-speed aircraft. In 1938, Hughes flew around the world in three days, 19 hours, and four minutes—breaking the record. After the Spruce Goose debacle, however, Hughes retreated from the public gaze and was rarely seen again. He died in 1975.

engineer Nick Burdon of Glyndŵr University in Great Britain fed the details of the Spruce Goose into a special

aviation computer program. It showed that the plane could have flown at 21,000 feet as designed, but the pilot would have had to be very careful to make gentle turns—otherwise the plane would spiral and crash.

Leaving aside some doubts about whether the plane actually "flew," we can use some basic science and engineering to work out why the Spruce Goose took so long to build. Remember that its purpose was to transport a huge load—75 tons, fully loaded. That weight demanded a lot of lift, the force that allows takeoff and keeps planes flying. And to provide lots of lift, you need big wings. That's why the H-4 Hercules still holds the record for the longest wingspan ever: 320 feet. You also need power, so each wing had four 3,000-horsepower engines.

Would it have all worked out faster and at far less cost if Hughes had been able to use those precious metals, rather than wood? Possibly, but it's more likely that the Spruce Goose was just too big to produce a flock of "Spruce Geese" that we'd still see flying.

PRESSURE DROP

Other planes built since the Spruce Goose have weighed more or been longer in length, but none has had a longer wingspan. You'll remember that the plane needed those giant wings to generate enough lift to get it aloft—and to keep it there.

You can do lots of experiments with fans and leaf blowers to demonstrate the principles that work to provide lift. Or . . . you could do a really simple experiment in the form of a challenge to your friends. It all depends on lift, although in this case the "lift" will be heading down. Confused? Well, things should become clearer once you accept this challenge.

YOU WILL NEED

- Some friends
- Piece of paper
- Scissors
- Table

METHOD

1. Tell your friends that you have a challenge: to blow a piece of paper off a table.

2 Fold the paper in half (so the crease is halfway between the long sides).

3 Use the scissors to cut the paper along that crease.

4 Take one of the half pieces and fold it one quarter of the way along the long side.

5 Do the same from the other end and fold the pieces over again so that they meet in the middle.

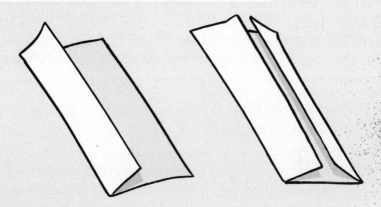

6 Unfold those flaps and place the paper on the table about a foot in from the edge; you should get it to stand up like a bridge if the flaps are down.

7 Ask a friend to blow along the top of the table to push the paper off. It should flatten against the table rather than be blown off.

CONTINUED

8 Now you take a turn blowing, but aim your breath (disguising its direction) just *above* the paper—it will fly right off!

WHAT'S UP?

When your friend blew, the air molecules sped quickly under the paper. When they pick up speed, they exert less pressure. That means that the air above the paper—which wasn't being blown and still had normal pressure—forced the paper down. And when you blew above the paper, the opposite happened and the paper flew away easily.

The same principle governs the design of airplane wings, although they're curved along the top. That curve speeds up the air as it passes *over* the wing, so that the difference in pressure forces it upward. And that's why lift is called "lift." With more wing to pass over—as with the Spruce Goose—there's more lift produced.

EXPERIMENT 19

"DRAG" RACING

Three of the most important forces linked to flight are lift, thrust, and drag. The first two forces work against the third to achieve flight. Drag is the big obstacle: Think of it as the wind in your face as you're riding your bike—it's trying to drag your speed down. A plane needs to overcome this drag with the lift that its wings provide, but they can't do their job unless the plane is moving forward. And that's where thrust from the engines comes in. It provides the power to move an aircraft forward so that the upward lift will overcome the drag holding it back.

A shape that cuts through the air—like a rocket or an arrow—reduces the drag of an object. But the H-4 Hercules had a huge fuselage because it had to hold so much cargo. The design had to overcome that problem by making huge wings (for more lift) and huge engines (for more thrust). Other aircraft designs go the other way—reducing drag with wings and engines that aren't so big. Try a few shapes in this experiment to see whether you might be an aviation designer one day.

YOU WILL NEED

> **Tall, clear pitcher**
> **Water**
> **Modeling clay (or play dough)**
> **Friend to help**
> **Stopwatch**

EXPERIMENT | 19

CONTINUED

METHOD

1 Fill the pitcher with water.

2 Break the clay into about 6 or more pieces, each about the size of a marble.

3 Form the clay pieces into different shapes. Be daring and make them as different as possible (for example, long tube, round, disk-shaped, teardrop).

4 Ask a friend to be your timer using the stopwatch.

5 Take a clay piece and hold it just at the water's surface, then ask your friend to time as you drop it into the water.

6 Stop timing when it hits the bottom.

7 Repeat Steps 4 to 6 with each piece of clay.

8 Compare how long each took to drop—the quickest had the least drag.

WHAT'S UP?

So why do this experiment in water if it's all about flight? That's because most of the laws that govern aviation (flight) apply to gases (like air) and liquids (like water) identically. The shape of the clay balls determines their drag whether they're sinking through a liquid or flying through the air. Aviation engineers do all sorts of tests like this one at the drawing board stage. Rounded or pointed-at-the-front shapes have the least drag because they can push aside air, just as you use your hand to slide curtains open.

CHAPTER 12

THE PLYWOOD SKYSCRAPER

Boston is known for its Colonial architecture, spacious parks, and attractive waterfront. It's not really famous for its skyscrapers like New York and Chicago are. In fact, some old-fashioned Bostonians believe that those high-rise buildings have no place crowding out their much-loved older buildings.

It took a special skyscraper to win Bostonians over: the John Hancock Tower. Standing 60 stories tall and rising 790 feet, it became Boston's tallest building when it was completed in 1976. Its shape was thin and graceful, and the mirrored windows were tinted slightly blue so that the building would seem to blend into the sky on clear days.

There was one small problem. Those 4- x 11-foot mirrored windows began falling off the building, each turning into 500 pounds of shattered glass on the ground below. In all, 65 panes fell out, and the skyscraper became dotted with plywood replacements. To make matters worse, people on the top floors began complaining of motion sickness—in a building?!

WHAT WENT WRONG?

THE "WINDOW problem" began in 1973, while the tower was still being built. A winter gale blew in on January 20, with gusts reaching 75 miles per hour. Sixty-five of the 10,344 windows came loose and fell to the ground.

For several years, some of the finest engineers at Massachusetts Institute of Technology (MIT) and Harvard University struggled to pinpoint what led to the problem. They installed sensitive instruments in the building, and MIT engineers built an entire scale model of the tower and surrounding neighborhood. They tested the model in a wind tunnel, trying to work out exactly how the wind affected the windows.

Back at the building, things were a bit more basic. Plywood sheets filled the gaps, and locals began calling it the "Plywood Palace" and "the tallest plywood skyscraper in the world." The building was roped off to protect people from falling windows whenever the wind reached 45 miles per hour. Janitors sat in chairs at street level at each corner, ready to blow whistles if they saw a pane of glass coming down.

WIND TUNNEL

A tube-shaped passage where engineers send a flow of air to study its effects on an object.

Engineers eventually solved the mystery of the falling windows, and the solution meant replacing every one of them. But even with the new windows secured in place, the tower was still a victim of the wind. One witness described the movement of the building as being like "a cobra's dance," moving forward and backward and twisting a little at the same time. That's when the people on the top floor started taking seasickness pills. The engineers then found a way to stop the rocking by "damping" the motion of the building.

THE MINIMALIST LOOK

I. M. Pei and Partners, the world-famous architects of the John Hancock Tower, designed the building in the minimalist style, which developed in the 1960s and 1970s. This style calls for sheer sides and a "minimum" of extra decoration, so the sides of the John Hancock Tower have no mullions (decorative window dividers) to go between the thousands of windows. The building looks like four tall, upright walls of glass.

The John Hancock Tower has now stood for decades without shedding windows or swaying drunkenly. Most young Bostonians think of it only as a graceful landmark, but older folks still go a little out of their way to avoid it if the wind starts to kick up!

TURN BACK THE CLOCK

AFTER ALL THE complicated studies in wind tunnels and labs, the engineers realized the windows were falling for a pretty basic reason. Each window was made up of two panes of glass, with a lead-tape spacer between them. Unfortunately, this spacer was forming *too* good a seal with the glass. Instead of allowing some breathing room to adjust to temperature changes, it just hung on tight, so when the glass reacted to heat or cold, the spacer didn't, and it plucked tiny bits of glass off. Pluck enough tiny bits and the seal breaks . . . and that's when the windows start to fall. The solution was drastic: Each of the 10,344 windows was replaced with single-paned, heat-treated glass.

INERTIA
The resistance of any object to a change in its motion.

Chicago might be called the Windy City, but Boston is actually the windiest city in the United States. That's where the next big problem came in. The strong wind was causing the John Hancock Tower to sway enough to give people on the top floors motion sickness. Local engineer William LeMessurier came up with a solution called a Tuned Mass Damper. Like a bridge damper (see page 103), it reduces the swaying. Two 300-ton weights were installed on the 58th floor. Each weight sits on a lubricated plate so that it can slide. The weights

are also connected by springs to the steel frame of the building. When the building sways, the floor moves under the weight, which wants to stay put because of inertia, and that's when the powerful springs kick in and tug the

building back. Since the installation of the damper, the tower has been stable—and its windows have remained in place.

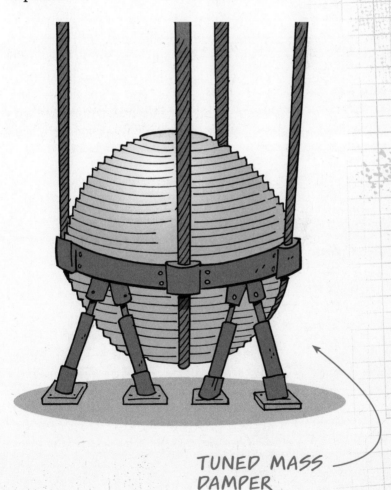

TUNED MASS DAMPER

BLOWING HOT AND COLD

The problem with the "Plywood Palace" in Boston turned out to be a seal that worked *too* well and didn't account for the effects of changing temperature on the glass panes and the air between them. Air molecules move around more when air is warmed up—that's what will happen to the air inside your submerged bottle here. While Boston has hot spells in the summer, the city suffers through some *really* cold periods each winter—as you'll see here with the bottle in the freezer. Do you think those John Hancock engineers knew about this basic principle—or were they too preoccupied with their minimalist designs to remember?

YOU WILL NEED

- ➤ **Sink or basin (as deep as the bottle is tall)**
- ➤ **Water**
- ➤ **Balloons**
- ➤ **2 empty 1-liter plastic bottles (and 1 cap)**
- ➤ **Freezer**

METHOD

1 Fill the sink or basin with water that's hot, but not too hot to touch.

2 Take a balloon and pull it this way and that to stretch it out a bit.

3 Feed the end of the balloon over the open top of one of the bottles.

4 Put the bottle into the water so it's submerged right up to the balloon.

5 Watch as the balloon fills up.

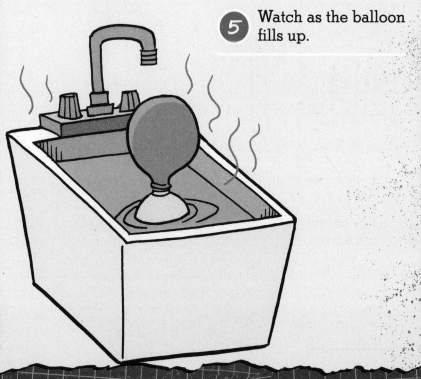

6 Screw the cap on the other bottle and put it in the freezer.

7 Remove the bottle after three hours and observe—the bottle will seem to have been crushed in on itself.

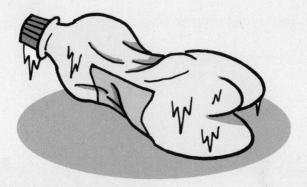

WHAT'S UP?

As with so many other problems we've examined in this book, something very basic—and seemingly insignificant—can cause *big* problems. You've seen here how air expands and contracts when it warms up and cools down. As the bottle warmed in the hot water, the air inside it became less dense and needed to find more space. That space, of course, was inside the balloon. The opposite happens as air cools: It contracts (takes up less space), and the sides of the bottle get pushed in to meet that smaller space of air inside. So air exerts a changing force on whatever is containing it, whether it's the panes of the John Hancock Tower's glass or a plastic bottle and balloon. Heating and cooling can affect other substances, like metal window frames, weakening the connections between them in a process called thermal stress.

INTO THE SWING

It was Sir Isaac Newton who came up with those famous Laws of Motion more than three centuries ago. He must have been impressed by the notion of inertia, because he defined it first: "An object either remains at rest or continues to move at a constant velocity [speed] unless an outside force acts on it."

That explains how someone could hit a softball in outer space and it would go on and on and on . . . because it would have no outside force like friction or gravity to slow it down. But it also explains why things that *aren't* moving don't want to budge. Think of those magicians who tug a tablecloth from under a table set with china plates and crystal glasses—ready to try out a version of that for yourself?

Here's a chance to reacquaint yourself with some of the fun that inertia can provide. And remember: This basic principle lies at the heart of the Hancock Tower's "cobra dance" problem. It's another case of going back to basics to solve a modern problem.

YOU WILL NEED

➤ **2 clear drinking glasses (not too flimsy; plastic if you're nervous)**
➤ **Water**
➤ **Several sheets of plain white paper**
➤ **Table**
➤ **2 caps from plastic bottles**
➤ **Eggs (hard-boiled if you're nervous)**

METHOD

1 Half fill the glasses with water.

2 Place them on a sheet of paper that's on the table; they should be near the far edge, with more paper on your side.

3 Carefully and firmly hold the near corners of the paper, calm yourself, and pull toward yourself quickly.

4 The glasses should remain standing where they were, with the paper now gone.

5 Now rest the sheet of paper over the glasses (if the paper's wet, use a dry one). Again, have more of it near you.

6 Place the bottle caps on the paper so that each rests over the center of the glass; the open bit of the caps should point up.

7 Put an egg upright (wider side down) in each cap so that each glass is covered by paper, then a cap, and then an egg.

8 Repeat Step 3—the caps should fly off but the eggs should drop into the glasses.

WHAT'S UP?

These quick demos are excellent examples of inertia. The glasses exhibited inertia when you pulled the paper from under them—just as the John Hancock Tower weights do when the floor slides beneath them. And of course, the more massive an object, the greater its inertia. That explains why the caps (with little mass) had a small amount of inertia and went flying but the more massive eggs stayed put. It also explains why the John Hancock Tower has two huge weights, each weighing 300 tons, to use inertia to stop the rocking.

CHAPTER 13

RADIAL TIRES COME UNGLUED

Radial tires arrived on the automotive scene in the early 1970s. They differed from the traditional bias ply tires in how the inner layers of rubber were designed and attached to each other. Many drivers were attracted to the radials' increased safety, better gas mileage, reduced vibration, and longer tread life. Automobile manufacturers began to choose them for their new cars, creating a demand for millions of these radials.

Two big tire manufacturers, Michelin and Goodrich, began leading the way in radial production, leaving rival Firestone Tire Company to play catchup. Firestone altered existing machinery to produce the Firestone 500 radials quickly, but their quality was patchy at best. Reports of high-speed blowouts, flipped cars, and fatal crashes began to mount up.

The company stubbornly refused to acknowledge any blame, but public outrage, fines, and lawsuits forced Firestone to recall 14.5 million of its first-generation radials. The cost: a whopping $150 million. How many lives and how much money could have been saved if the company had acted differently?

WHAT WENT WRONG?

THE ARRIVAL OF radial tires around 1970 signaled a new chapter in automotive design and engineering. Until then, engineers had busied themselves with engine technology, fuel-supply improvements, reducing air resistance, electronics, and a range of constantly updated automotive features inside and out. Radials showed that the same level of attention to tires could produce a better-engineered product.

The Firestone Company was slow to pick up on the trend and began to "tool up" for this new generation of tires in late 1971. Not long after, Firestone began having trouble with the bonding of the rubber compounds (mixtures) that would stick the outer layer (the tread) with the brass-coated steel wire of the inner layers. Water could seep into these gaps, causing the metal to rust and the layers to come apart along the sidewalls—sometimes at highway speeds.

Reports of accidents—many of them fatal—were traced to the Firestone 500 radials. Soon there were enough people seeking legal damages from Firestone for injuries and deaths that the federal government began investigating radial tires. But Firestone stubbornly continued to produce and sell the tires, even after the National Highway Traffic Safety Administration (NHTSA) began investigating, too. In November 1977, the Center for Auto Safety urged Firestone to recall its "500" radials.

TOOL UP

To prepare for a new process by adding new equipment.

Pressure was building from many sides on Firestone, but the company continued to claim that any problems were due to poor driving and not poor manufacturing. Firestone only backed down when a special

WHEN IT BLOWS

When a tire suddenly loses its tread—as happened with so many of the Firestone 500 radials—the vehicle becomes unstable and hard to control, especially at high speeds. The result is what police and road-safety experts call "single vehicle crashes," because other vehicles are usually not involved. The loss of control of just one wheel can cause a vehicle to roll over. By the mid-1970s, only the most foolhardy of Firestone 500 owners would have ignored the warning signs of a developing bulge in the sidewall area and an audible thumping noise.

committee of the House of Representatives held open hearings about the tires in July 1978. Firestone was forced to pay a $500,000 fine and to recall 14.5 million of the Firestone 500 radials.

SIDEWALL

The part of a tire between the edge of the tread and the rim of the wheel.

TURN BACK THE CLOCK

THE CASE OF THE Firestone 500 recall is a special one. In fact, students at Harvard Business School and other business schools study the Firestone 500 story to learn how *not* to manage a company in a crisis. (At least it was good for something!)

The first poor decision was to jump the gun and begin producing radial tires on modified equipment designed for bias-ply tires. Firestone was producing radials by the start of 1971, but the quality was poor, and it was hard to train workers to operate these altered machines.

By 1972, the company had also become aware that the adhesive to bind the different tire layers was imperfect. Reports of accidents were common, but the company continued to produce tires that seemed untested. Firestone publicly ignored or played down criticisms of its radials and accusations that it was using the American public as guinea pigs to test its products. At the same time, Firestone was trying to settle any legal cases quickly and quietly.

ADHESIVE

A substance used to stick objects or materials together.

The situation continued in much the same way for several years. It only came to a head when the House of Representative's Interstate & Foreign Commerce Committee demanded the recall of the Firestone 500 radials in 1978.

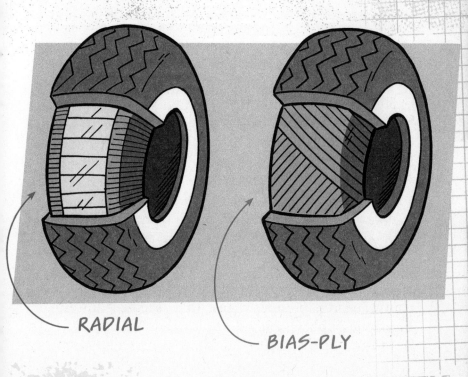

RADIAL

BIAS-PLY

WHAT'S IN A RADIAL TIRE?

Modern tires have a network of cords, called plies, to give them strength. On some tires, particularly older ones, two layers of ply (one inside the other) run diagonally across the tire, forming a letter *X*. That is the arrangement on bias-ply tires. The plies on radial tires go straight across the tire, as if they had *radiated* out from the center of the wheel. This arrangement of plies provides flexibility. Radial tires also have rigid steel belts to reinforce the tire tread. Part of the Firestone problem stemmed from the poor-quality adhesive attaching the rubber to the brass-coated steel wire of the plies.

CORROSION DAMAGE

The failure of the Firestone 500's bonding material (to join layers together) created gaps between the layers. Water was able to enter those gaps and act on the steel bands that were meant to provide strength and support for the tires. Water, air, and metals such as steel combine to create a chemical reaction called oxidation, which we know as either corrosion or rust. Metal gets weaker when it rusts—as you'll see in this experiment.

The demo calls for steel wool. However, the steel wool that you can buy in most supermarkets (for washing pots and pans) has probably been treated with antirust chemicals, and that would get you nowhere. Instead, buy your steel wool from a hardware store and choose the finest grade available—it will rust more quickly.

YOU WILL NEED

- 2 steel wool pads
- Wide-mouthed glass jar with a lid (one that's for recycling—not one that you need to keep)
- White vinegar
- Rubber gloves
- Paper towel
- Plain white paper

METHOD

1 Put 1 steel wool pad in the jar, cover it with vinegar, and screw the lid back on. Leave it overnight.

2 The next day, open the jar with gloves on, pour the liquid down the drain, and carefully remove the steel wool pad.

3 Set the steel wool pad on a sheet of paper towel to let it dry for about 20 minutes.

4 Lay the sheet of paper on the table.

5 Pick up the second steel wool pad (the one that wasn't soaking) and hold it over the paper.

CONTINUED

6 Flick it several times and observe the paper below—there shouldn't be much landing on it.

7 Put the gloves back on and repeat Step 6 with the first pad that's been drying—you should see lots of flecks.

WHAT'S UP?

You've just done two experiments in one. The first was to get the steel to corrode (or rust). It would do that even if it had soaked in water, but vinegar acts as a catalyst. That's something that makes a chemical reaction—like corrosion—go faster. The corrosion process means that bits of the metal either dissolve or flake off, leaving the metal much weaker (think of rusty nails falling out of wood). The metal bands of the Firestone 500 radial tires also rusted, becoming weaker and eventually giving way.

SPINNING OUT

The constant spinning of an automobile wheel creates a lot of stress on the layers of the tire. Two forces are working against each other the whole time—one drawing the layers in (centripetal) and another trying to let them fly off (centrifugal). Sticking the layers of tires together is an adhesive that helps balance these forces, but the constant stress on the adhesive might make it fail, with disastrous results for the vehicle, driver, and passengers.

Here's a demonstration of the forces at work on any spinning object, giving you a good idea of what went wrong with those faulty tires.

YOU WILL NEED

- ➤ **Friends to watch and take part in the quiz**
- ➤ **Jump rope with wooden handles**

TAKE CARE!

You really need a lot of space to do this experiment, so it's best to find a park or a big yard.

METHOD

1 Make sure your friends are at a safe distance.

2 Face them and hold one jump rope handle in one hand and grasp the rope about 18 inches away from it with the other hand. The other handle should be clear of the ground—lift up the rope if it isn't.

3 Move the hand that's holding the rope up and down quickly so that the longer length of jump rope starts swinging in a circle vertically.

CONTINUED

4 Ask your friends what will happen if you let go of the rope when the handle is at the very top of the circle. (Most people say that it will go straight up.)

5 Continue swinging and then let go when it is at the top: The handle will shoot sideways, not straight up.

WHAT'S UP?

Most people get the wrong end of the stick when they think about the forces at work on spinning objects. They believe that something called centrifugal force is pushing straight out from the center of the circle, driving the spinning object in that same "straight out" direction. But your demonstration just proved otherwise.

The spinning object *is* trying to continue in a straight line, but not a straight line out from the center. That's because a different force, called centripetal force, constantly draws it in. When the centripetal force is reduced or lost, the object does go flying straight off in the direction it was just traveling.

A satellite, for example, continues to travel around the Earth rather than fly off into space because gravity provides the centripetal force that draws it in. Your firm hand on the rope provided a similar force while you were twirling, and so did the tire's adhesive (while it held). But you lessened the centripetal force by letting go of the rope. The centripetal force of the Firestone 500 tires was lost when the adhesive failed: The outer layer (tread) went flying straight off in the form of a blowout. And that's when the vehicle got into real trouble.

CHAPTER 14

WHOOPS— THE LAKE'S GONE

Lake Peigneur, Louisiana, looked like someone's daydream about the pleasures of country living. Pecan trees and live oaks along the shore rustled in a light breeze. Out on the lake, Leonce Viator and his nephew were going for catfish when they noticed that their boat started moving.

The two fishermen looked out in surprise—then horror—when they realized that they were being drawn toward a whirlpool that was growing bigger by the second. Everything was happening fast as they swirled around the hole again and again. Two barges disappeared before Leonce managed to tie his boat to a tree jutting up through the water.

Within seconds, the water had drained away from the base of the tree and the lake bed was now exposed. The fishermen scrambled to the safety of the "real" shore and looked back. Boats, logs, trees, and even an island had been sucked away. All of this was bizarre, but it was just part of the story of "the world's weirdest engineering disaster."

WHAT WENT WRONG?

LAKE PEIGNEUR lies in a part of southern Louisiana teeming with underground riches, like oil and salt. On November 20, 1980, the oil company Texaco began drilling test holes through the base of the shallow lake to find possible oil reserves deep underground. The 14-inch-wide drill bore deeper and deeper, and then got stuck at a depth of 1,228 feet. The crew couldn't remove it or even get it to budge.

As the crew puzzled over the problem, the drill began to tilt and sink into the lake. Seconds later, the whole $5 million rig followed it down. Miraculously, the crew scrambled to safety. They joined onlookers on the shore as an entire landscape changed in front of them. Everything in and around the lake—boats, docks, precious semitropical trees—was sucked into the giant whirlpool. Within hours the lake was drained, although it would refill in a couple of days—with salt water. What had caused this dreadful turn of events? Could an engineering mistake *really* drain 3.5 billion gallons of water?

You bet it could—in triangulating where to drill, Texaco engineers used faulty data and ended up about 400 feet off target. Instead of drilling down through solid rock and into possible oil reserves, they headed straight into a salt mine that lay beneath the lake. Water rushed from the lake down through the drill hole and into the cavernous mine below. As the rushing water dissolved more salt,

TRIANGULATION

A method of establishing the location of a fixed point based from the angles to it from two other points along a fixed line.

the hole got wider and wider, the flow got faster, and the whirlpool grew bigger. Like their oil-rig counterparts on the lake surface, the 50 miners deep below made a daring emergency escape.

FROM FRESH TO SALT

Lake Peigneur covered about two square miles but was only about 10 feet deep—which is why the oil workers must have been shocked to see their huge rig disappear. The mine below was an enormous cavern held up by salt columns. When these columns dissolved, the cavern collapsed, sending air rushing up through the widening drill hole, and briefly creating a 400-foot geyser (a column of water pushed upward by pressure from below). An adjoining canal, whose water level had originally been the same as the lake's, then flowed into the drained lake. The current was so strong that it drew water from the Gulf of Mexico, turning Lake Peigneur into a saltwater lake.

TURN BACK THE CLOCK

THE TEXACO BOSSES had known about the salt mine and so they would have also known what should happen if they drilled straight into it. That part of Louisiana had lots of rich pockets of oil underground, and a number of oil wells were near the lake. The Diamond Crystal Salt Company would have known exactly where its mine was and warned the oil people. Somewhere in the chain of communication from "Avoid this area!" to "Let's get drilling!" the drill was misdirected.

It's hard to say who made that fundamental mistake because all the machinery and records were lost in the accident, but the way that the mistake was made is clear: It was poor triangulation, a skill that good engineers and surveyors know like the back of their hand. It's a neat way of finding a third point if you know exactly where two other points are. Just think of the word "triangle," and you'll get an idea of how it works. With a good head for math and the right equipment, an engineer can find that third point accurately. Except back in November 1980, when some of those calculations must have been mixed up and workers started drilling 400 feet away— right over the salt mine!

Could anyone have expected that the lake—along with just about everything on or near it—would vanish "down the drain"? Well, they might have if they knew something about the power of a vortex, where spinning water flows down quickly.

You've probably seen water do that when you drain the bathtub: As it gets closer to the plug hole, the water picks up speed and spins faster and faster. That's just what the water in Lake Peigneur started to do as it flowed down into the salt mine. It formed a spinning funnel about the size of a tornado—with some of the same energy—pulling almost everything down with it.

WHAT—NO EVIDENCE?

What happened in those few hours of November 20, 1980, is clear in everyone's memory—the draining lake, the missing barges (some of which reemerged when the lake filled up again), the geyser, the redirected canal. But just about everything we know about the events *before* that fateful drilling relies on the testimony of those involved. The actual machinery and paperwork records of the calculations—which could prove who made the fateful mistake—went "down the drain" with the drilling rig.

THE VIOLENT VORTEX

You might have seen this experiment performed before as a way of demonstrating how whirlpools form, but it's also just like what happened in Lake Peigneur in 1980. The fresh water from the lake drained down through the hole that the drill made—think of that being the water rushing through the hole connecting the bottle tops here. Hold on tight because you are about to create a whirlpool—or to use the scientific term, a vortex.

YOU WILL NEED

> ➤ **2 empty identical soda bottles with caps (large bottles work best)**
> ➤ **Adult**
> ➤ **Sharp knife**
> ➤ **Electrical tape**
> ➤ **Water**
> ➤ **Food coloring (optional)**

METHOD

1 Remove all the labels from the soda bottles.

2 Remove the bottle caps and ask an adult to use the knife to cut a hole about ½-inch wide in each of them.

3 Tape the bottle caps together tightly, flat side to flat side. Be generous with the tape (about 4 layers).

4 Fill one of the bottles about two-thirds full of water. (Add a few drops of food coloring if you want.)

CONTINUED

5 Screw the bottle-top combination onto that bottle and then screw the other empty bottle (upside down) onto the bottle top that's pointing up.

6 Turn the combination over, and the water will start to gurgle and drain irregularly, or maybe hardly at all. (You might need to hold the lower bottle to keep it secure.)

7 Pick up the bottle combination and move it in a swirling motion.

8 Carefully place the combination down again with the full bottle on top (it might stand on its own) and you'll see a dramatic whirlpool draining out.

WHAT'S UP?

When the water inside the bottles is still, the combination of surface tension (at the mouth of the top bottle) and air pressure (in the lower bottle) means that very little water flows down. But when you twirl the bottles, the water begins to spin, creating a hole in the middle of the spinning water. The hole allows air to move into the top bottle, which also lets the spinning water flow down into the lower bottle. As the water descends from thicker to narrower sections of the bottle, it begins to spin faster—just like draining a bathtub or a figure skater twirling faster when she draws her arms in near her body. This combination of downward and circular motion is called a vortex. The vortex in Lake Peigneur was powerful enough to drain the lake!

CHAPTER 15

THE SINCLAIR C5 STALLS

Englishman Sir Clive Sinclair was a man with a glowing reputation. In the early 1980s, he was familiar to most British people. They saw him as an inventor, a businessman, a visionary, and even a genius. Sinclair was always at the cutting edge of technology, having developed some of the earliest handheld calculators and home computers.

In January 1985, he launched one of his most ambitious projects to date—the Sinclair C5, a single-passenger electric vehicle that seemed ideal for city travel. Reporters and television crews were present as the vehicle was unveiled. But a winter launch proved to be a bad call: Observers chuckled as they watched newly purchased C5s skidding on snow and ice or hidden by trucks in heavy traffic. Sales for the C5 slowed down, and complaints came in of poor steering, lack of power, bad headlights, and discomfort from the lights of oncoming vehicles.

By October 1985, the company producing the C5 was closed. Britain's resident genius had finally come up with a dud. How did things go so badly wrong? And would it mean "the end of the road" for the future of electric cars?

WHAT WENT WRONG?

PEOPLE IN THE 1980s were finally beginning to take an interest in recycling, reducing energy consumption, and cutting down on pollution. Many could also remember the fuel shortages and skyrocketing price of gasoline in the 1970s. So an electric vehicle that promised travel at almost no cost—and no pollution—pressed all the right buttons. An even bigger plus, it seemed, was the C5's inventor. Sir Clive Sinclair was a self-made millionaire who had amassed a fortune with ingenious electronic products and inventions, so his reputation was certainly high—and on the line.

In the early 1980s, Sinclair designed a three-wheeled battery-powered electric vehicle that also had pedals to

SINCLAIR

help on steeper climbs. It was low to the ground, 2½ feet wide and high, and 6 feet 9 inches long. It had front and rear lights and a small trunk. The battery, which took eight hours to charge, would provide a top speed of 15 miles per hour on level ground. The total weight, including the battery, was 99 pounds.

The Sinclair C5 should have given people the freedom to dash off to town, do some shopping or grab a slice of pizza, and head home—all for the cost of a few pennies. But problems began to mount up. The vehicle had no roof (in rainy Britain, of all places), and being so low down meant that drivers often wound up directly behind the exhaust pipes of other cars. Plus drivers had to order special poles that would stick up and alert truck drivers that there was a tiny vehicle down there somewhere.

TURNING CIRCLE

The diameter of the circle (more accurately, semicircle) that a vehicle needs to make in order to do a U-turn.

Pedaling uphill was a chore for many people, especially when the vehicle had just one gear—try riding your bike up a steep hill in the highest gear and then imagine doing it with something that weighed nearly 100 pounds! A wide turning circle and lack of a reverse gear made the C5 hard to maneuver. Customers also complained that their batteries rarely reached their 20-mile range, often conking out after 10 miles or less in the cold.

The writing was on the wall for the Sinclair C5 before it even reached the end of its first winter. Clive Sinclair's reputation took a hammering, and only 5,000 of the 14,000 vehicles produced were sold. Production stopped in August 1985 and Sinclair Vehicles (the company that produced the C5) closed down for good.

TURN BACK THE CLOCK

SIR CLIVE SINCLAIR might have shown his genius in giving the world portable calculators and home computers, but he seemed to lose his golden touch with the C5. Three decades on, some people say that he was just ahead of his time and that 21st-century drivers are much more eager to try electric or hybrid cars. The world certainly needs low-pollution cars more than ever, but the C5 had few of the comforts and advantages of today's full-size hybrid automobiles.

A few changes at the time would have improved life for C5 drivers. The vehicle absolutely needed to have some sort of covering or roof to protect the driver from the elements. Better covering could also have protected drivers from exhaust fumes coming at them at head level.

Sinclair should have developed a set of gears—like normal bicycle gears—as a standard feature to make climbing easier. Likewise, the high-visibility mast (which had only been an option back in 1985) should have been fitted to every C5. The sense of being invisible to other drivers turned many potential buyers off at the time of the vehicle's launch.

The Sinclair C5 also would have been a better product if its steering had been improved so that its turning circle was reduced. That change, plus the introduction of a reverse electric gear, would have made it much easier to maneuver.

The most important modern change would be to use an improved battery. In the last few

> ## HYBRID
> A vehicle that has both an electric motor and a gasoline-powered engine, either of which can propel it.

decades, batteries have become smaller and more powerful. A modern battery would weigh half as much and provide more than twice as much range and power—which would have certainly helped on those hills. Today's environmentally friendly electric and hybrid automobiles have successfully earned a growing share of the market. Sinclair's "failure" has actually inspired much of this success, since manufacturers learned from the mistakes. The measures taken to improve on the C5 should help the health of the planet in the long run.

SILVER LINING?

Some of the people who bought Sinclair C5s back in 1985 and then stored them in their garages for 30 years might be in for a pleasant surprise. Collectors are showing a lot of interest in these "failures," just as American dealers are looking for Edsels (a Ford "flop" from the late 1950s). Used C5s in good condition now fetch more than three times their original price.

TAKING THINGS WIDE

You might wonder what the big deal is about a turning circle. Well, not only does it help the driver snuggle into a tight parking space, it sometimes means the difference between being able to turn around in a narrow street or having to back up all the way. And don't forget that the Sinclair C5 was pretty heavy and had no reverse gear.

Here's a demonstration of turning circles that you can test yourself, using the widest collection of bikes that you can find.

YOU WILL NEED

- Baseball card or similar-size card
- Friends to ride bikes
- As many bicycles as possible (with wheels of different sizes)
- Watering can full of water
- Tape measure

TAKE CARE!

You'll need some open space to do this experiment. Try to find a safe part of a parking lot or even some space in a park (if they allow bikes).

1. You'll be measuring the diameter of a circle, so mark the center of it by putting the baseball card down on the ground.

2. Water the front tire of each person's bike before their turn so that their track will show up.

3. Ask each friend (who'll be riding one of the different bikes) to ride up slowly to the card and then do a U-turn by turning clockwise. The winner is the rider with the narrowest turning circle.

4 Anyone who puts a foot down is disqualified.

5 Use the tape measure to decide between close results.

6 Discuss how and why the winner won. Does it tell you anything about how the wheel size affects the turning circle?

WHAT'S UP?

Okay, so you've had a bit of fun comparing how tightly you and your friends can make a U-turn, and you have a firsthand experience of what a turning circle is. Now stop for a minute and imagine your grandmother stuck in a dead-end street, trying to get her Sinclair C5 back to the main road. Does the idea of wanting a tighter turning circle seem a little more understandable now? And can you think of anything that the designers could have done with the C5's wheels to "tighten" that circle?

ONWARD AND UPWARD?

This combination activity/experiment lets you make your own tabletop wagon, which you'll power with an energy source—the air from a hair dryer. You'll see just how effective that energy source is in powering the wagon on varying slopes and flat surfaces based on the size and shape of different sails. You're looking for the ideal shape to harness the same force to propel the wagon as far as possible.

Remember those slopes that proved to be a big obstacle for the Sinclair C5? The battery didn't have enough power to push it up a lot of hills, and the "pedal it yourself" feature of the C5 wasn't all that user-friendly. With a more powerful—or more efficient—battery, it might have made those climbs.

YOU WILL NEED

> Three 4- x 6-inch index cards
> Clear tape
> 3 plastic straws
> Life Savers (or similar round candy)
> Scissors
> Several sheets of plain white paper
> Mounting putty (or play dough)
> Tape measure
> Hair dryer

METHOD

1 Stack the index cards and tape them together using about ½ inch of tape along each side of the cards. (Three layers taped together will add strength to the mini-wagon you're making.)

2 Put the stack on the floor and place a straw across the narrower side, about ½ inch in from the edge and jutting out the same distance from each side.

3 Stick the straw in place with tape at both ends.

4 Slide a Life Saver onto both jutting ends and then wrap tape around the straws just outside the candies; these will be the wheels, so make sure they can turn and that there's just enough tape to stop them from sliding off the straw.

5 Use the scissors to cut the straw so just a bit of it (covered in tape) juts out beyond the candy.

6 Repeat Steps 2 to 5 at the other end. You now have a wagon that can roll.

CONTINUED

7 Cut the plain white paper into different-size shapes (maybe a circle, rectangle, triangle, and diamond) and cut two ½-inch slits in each shape; the slits should be midway across each shape, about ½ inch from the top and bottom edges.

8 Each of those shapes will be used as a sail for the wagon. Each time you need a sail, you slide the third straw (the "mast") through the 2 slots and pinch the paper a little so that it forms a curve.

9 Put a small blob of mounting putty on the top of the wagon (the side without the straw "axles" running across it); it should be about an inch in front of the center of the card.

10 Mount a mast and straw on the wagon and place it on a hard floor.

11 Use the tape measure to line up the hair dryer exactly 30 inches behind the wagon and turn it on to low; mark where the wagon finishes.

12 Repeat Steps 10 and 11 with all your shapes, noting how far each wagon travels.

WHAT'S UP?

This uses scientific methods even if it seems to be just a lot of hot air and fun. The force that you or your friends apply to the wagon to power it is constant (because you remained the same distance away each time). That's your power output—just as vehicles have a power output in the form of the engine, or battery in the case of the C5.

By changing the shape or size of the sail, you're trying to get the most force (from the dryer) to power the wagon, but too much would tip it over. The scientific method kicks in as you compare how the same power output can produce different results. A larger sail harnesses more of that power up to a "tipping point." The C5 engineers also experimented with maximizing power output—their methods led to bigger, heavier batteries, but the extra weight offset that advantage.

CHAPTER 16

THE EXXON VALDEZ OIL SPILL

On March 23, 1989, the 987-foot *Exxon Valdez* set sail from Valdez in southern Alaska, bound for Long Beach, California. It was the second-newest of Exxon's 20-ship fleet, and similar vessels had safely shipped oil 8,700 times since the Trans-Alaska Pipeline had opened 12 years earlier. No one expected trouble, especially with the calm seas.

So when disaster struck three hours later around midnight, it was shocking. The ship had run aground on a reef, rupturing its hold full of oil. Before the flow could be stopped, about 11 million gallons had leaked into the coastal Pacific waters. It was an environmental catastrophe that would foul the fragile coastline, killing hundreds of thousands of sea animals—and its effects would last well into the new century. How did it happen, how could it have been prevented, and can that stretch of beautiful coastline ever recover?

HUGE TANKERS

ship Alaska's crude oil from the port of Valdez, about 70 miles east of Anchorage, to refineries all around the world. On the evening of March 23, 1989, the *Exxon Valdez* was about to set off on just such a voyage to Long Beach, California, about 2,200 miles south along the Pacific Coast.

At about 11:20 p.m., the ship had safely navigated the tricky Valdez Narrows. Captain Joe Hazelwood spotted some icebergs in the normal shipping lanes and steered the ship onto a new course. He handed the navigation of the ship to third mate Gregory Cousins, ordering him to return to the shipping lanes as soon as the ship reached a certain point.

For reasons that are still a mystery, that never happened. (Some reports said that Captain Hazelwood had been drinking alcohol before the ship departed.) The ship continued outside the safe shipping lanes and then, just after midnight, the crew heard several sharp sounds before the vessel drew to a halt. It had hit Bligh Reef at 12:04 a.m. on March 24. Eight of its 11 cargo holds had been pierced, and 11 million gallons of oil began flowing directly into the sea.

The effects of the spill were dramatic. Countless fish died and washed up ashore, covered in oil. Seabirds were also victims, with as many as 250,000 dying, along with 2,800 sea otters, 300 harbor seals, 247 bald eagles, and 22 orca whales. The alert for a massive cleanup operation went out almost immediately, and soon teams lined the shores, using different methods to contain the oil and save the wildlife.

Teams of boats towing long booms and skimmers tried to get oil from the surface of the water, but they were limited by bad

BOOM

A long U-shaped metal bar towed behind two boats to gather up oil after a spill.

weather conditions and lack of supplies. High-pressure hoses blasted hot water against oil-covered rocks along the shore, although some experts believe that these methods killed many of the microorganisms that could have helped clear up the oil naturally.

The effects of the oil spill have lingered for nearly three decades, with some areas still suffering from the decline of wildlife. Exxon had to pay more than $1 billion in fines and compensation, in addition to money it spent on its own cleanup efforts.

SKIMMER

A device that fits onto the curve of a boom to collect oil, working like a sieve.

TURN BACK THE CLOCK

IF WE'RE TRYING to avoid more *Exxon Valdez* disasters—and experts have been hard at it since 1989—we need to consider how ship design and cleanup operations can improve. On one hand, we can point to the 8,700 safe trips out of Valdez that preceded the *Exxon Valdez* disaster and conclude that regulations and standard practices were very effective. That view puts the blame squarely on human error—how the captain and crew behaved on the night. Had the captain drunk alcohol? Was the crew poorly trained? Did Exxon make everyone work too many hours and get tired?

On the other hand, some observers argue that even if human error had been mainly to blame, ships themselves should be better protected from the gashes that cause spills, anyway. One solution is double hulls. Some cargo ships load their goods directly into the hull (the main body of the ship), which becomes the only layer between cargo and sea. A double hull adds another layer inside, with a gap between the layers. In theory, such an arrangement offers double protection. But the extra hull also affects how the ship rides in the water, possibly affecting its stability . . . running the risk of making it capsize and lose even *more* oil. Tricky!

What about ways to improve cleanup operations? The exact methods that are used depend on the circumstances—weather conditions, overall temperature, human and animal populations nearby, and many other factors. Some of the methods used in 1989 are still useful in many oil spills. If conditions are favorable, the oil can actually be burned off the

DISPERSANT

A chemical, such as a detergent, that clusters around tiny drops of oil and allows them to be carried away (dispersed) in the water.

water's surface in places, though in high winds, this technique can cause pollution. Chemical dispersants allow oil to be carried away by ocean currents, but dispersant-oil droplets can sometimes sink and damage life on the seafloor. Bioremediation uses tiny microorganisms such as bacteria to break down or even eat the oil. This could be a way of cleaning up disastrous messes without creating even more air or water pollution.

OIL

DOUBLE HULL

DOUBLE HULLS

The *Exxon Valdez* was equipped with a double bottom—an extra layer of ship's hull inside the main hull. It was meant to provide protection against piercings from below, such as it might receive from submerged rocks. People argue even now about whether having a double hull—a second layer not only along the bottom but up both sides—would have helped matters.

The trouble with double hulls is that they fix one problem (rocks and icebergs) but create another (reducing a ship's stability in the water). This simple experiment shows you how and why. You might need to try different combinations of plastic cups to get it to work, but the result is an eye-opener.

YOU WILL NEED

> **Sink or bucket**
> **Water**
> **Small plastic cup (that can fit inside the large cup, but not too snugly)**
> **Large plastic cup with no handle (about 8 fluid ounces)**

METHOD

1 Plug the sink and fill it about two-thirds high with water.

2 Fill the small cup with water and pour it into the large cup.

3 Carefully place this large cup in the water-filled sink and note how well it stays upright; if it's tipping, try adding another ½ cup of water from the small cup to it.

4 Take the large cup from the water and pour out its water.

5 Fill the smaller cup with water and place it carefully inside the larger cup.

6 Now place this combination of cups (your "double-hull tanker") in the sink and let go, noting how stable it is.

WHAT'S UP?

Usually the "double-hull" cup rocks more and often capsizes—compared with the single-hull version that can hold more. That's because the second hull raises the center of mass (the point where the mass of the object is most concentrated) higher up, making the vessel less stable. Ships are more stable with a lower center of mass. But just like so many engineering issues, there's a trade-off involved. The second hull provides more protection against piercing, but it can have negative effects on how seaworthy the ship becomes.

THE PARIS AIRPORT COLLAPSE

Airports in national capitals are far more than places to pass through on your way up to the skies. They also tell the world about the entire country that they serve.

The designers of Charles de Gaulle Airport outside Paris assumed that people knew about France's centuries of history, its great works of art and architecture, and, above all, its wonderful food (snails and frogs legs included). But they wanted to show the world that France is also a modern country, so they made the futuristic Terminal 2E, which opened in June 2003, the showpiece.

The curving glass and concrete design combined beauty with high-tech efficiency, and millions of travelers thought it looked like a space station. This was a bold statement by an airport aiming to overtake London and Frankfurt as Europe's most important. But in May 2004, a huge slab of curved concrete crashed onto the terminal floor, killing four people. What led to this disaster, and what can an airport do if its own terminal collapses?

WHAT WENT WRONG?

AIRPORT TERMINALS do a lot of things besides providing a place for planes to dock so passengers can board or exit the aircraft. Terminals also need luggage transport, ticket counters, security, customs, shops, restaurants, restrooms . . . the list goes on! The main feature is movement, and it's important that the terminal allows people to move freely.

All of those are the basic building blocks of airport terminal design. Charles de Gaulle Airport executives asked world-famous Paul Andreu, their chief architect since 1967, to combine these ingredients for Terminal 2E. He produced a design for a long, tubelike passage connecting 2E to other terminals. The terminal took the shape of a wide, flattened vault that curved gracefully over the concourse. Curving concrete formed the inside of the vault, with rectangular holes to let light flood in. The outside of the terminal was a great sweeping curve of glass, following and covering the shape of the concrete inside. Metal struts—structural supports to resist downward pressure—linked the glass layer on the outside with the concrete inside.

VAULT

A large room with an arch-shaped ceiling.

CONCOURSE

A large open area inside a public building.

The effect was dramatic, with light splashing across the wide expanses of floor. That open area, uninterrupted by posts or columns to hold the roof up, added to the overall effect of light and space—exactly the futuristic look that Andreu dreamed of. Instead, the vault rested on relatively few low columns along the sides of the concrete.

Terminal 2E had been operating for just under a year when on May 23, 2004, an enormous 100-foot section of the concrete and glass vault collapsed, killing four people. The death toll would have been much worse if the airport had been more crowded—it came down at 7 a.m. on a quiet Sunday. French officials closed the terminal to conduct a detailed investigation, and it would remain shuttered for nearly four years. The repair project, costing 100 million euros (about $125 million), replaced the concrete and glass vault with a more traditional steel and glass section.

TURN BACK THE CLOCK

TWO TERMS THAT crop up over and over again in engineering and design are "form" and "function." When a design is boiled down to its basics, it needs to provide a balance between them. Form describes how something looks—like how graceful it seems, or how it blends in with its surroundings. Function is all about the job that a building needs to do. For instance, some people find the appearance (form) of plate-glass skyscrapers dull or ugly, but those buildings score high on function because they use space efficiently.

Paul Andreu, as an experienced airport architect, knew all about the function of an airport terminal, but he may have relied a bit too much on form when creating the impression of bright, airy space in the Terminal 2E design. The investigation after the crash noted that there was a big price to pay for a building that looked as though it just hung in the air: It might just fall down! Investigators reported that the building would have been far more secure if it had used some internal supports like floor-to-ceiling columns, even if they broke up the uninterrupted space of the concourse.

Such floor-to-ceiling columns—or supports extending from outward from the roof and downward to the ground—are examples of safety features known as redundant supports. "Redundant" is an odd word for designers to use, because it sometimes means "extra, and not necessary." A better word might be "backup" or "failsafe" in case something fails or is destroyed. That gives you a better idea of how these extra supports—which might never be needed—could become lifesavers if a column does collapse.

The terminal collapsed in a sort of chain reaction. Investigators concluded that the metal attached to the outside glass layer—and the metal struts connecting to the inner concrete layer—expanded and contracted (shrank) as the temperature outside rose and fell. This swelling and shrinking of the metal weakened the concrete until it gave way with deadly consequences that Sunday morning.

LEARNING FROM OTHERS' MISTAKES

The Dulles Corridor Metrorail Project is an ambitious plan to link many areas of Virginia, Maryland, and Washington, DC. Early plans called for similar vaulted spaces in the Tysons Corner station (part of the Metrorail network). After the events at Terminal 2E, though, an official study urged caution about repeating the French mistakes, and in the end, the station plans were altered. Sturdy and "functional" concrete pillars took the place of soaring vaults in the no-nonsense new design.

METAL EXPANSION

French investigators noted that the weather had been pretty wacky in the days leading up to the airport's collapse. In particular, the temperature had been like a yo-yo, going from as low as 40°F to as high as 70°F. That heating and cooling caused the metal struts to expand and contract, which in turn weakened the connection with the inner concrete layer.

We find it hard to imagine this effect on hard, sturdy materials such as metals, but you can do a really quick experiment to see it in action. Plus, you might use the results to convince your family that you have the superhuman power to open any jar in the world!

YOU WILL NEED

> 2 identical empty glass jars with metal screw-top lids (jelly or pickle jars are ideal)
> Sink
> Cold running water
> Hot running water

METHOD

1 Tighten both lids firmly so you'd need to use most of your strength to open them.

2 Put one of the jars in the sink and run it under cold water for 30 seconds, then try to open it (it should still be hard or even harder to open).

3 Replace that jar with the second jar and run it under hot water for 30 seconds—be careful not to get splashed.

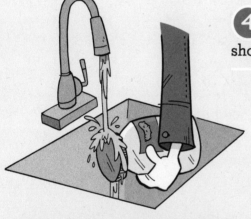

4 Now try to open this second jar; it should open easily.

WHAT'S UP?

The metal in the lids and the glass of the jars—like everything else in the world, including Terminal 2E's metal struts—is made up of atoms. These atoms vibrate more when they are heated. That extra vibration creates more space between the atoms, so the metal expands a little. Metal lids do just that, getting a little bigger. They do just the opposite when they cool. Some materials, such as glass or the concrete in Terminal 2E, don't expand quite as much. That means that the glass "stayed behind" a little while the metal lids moved away, getting looser.

CHILE'S TRAPPED MINERS

For 69 days in 2010, the world held its breath as it followed the story of a remote mine in Chile. Newspaper reporters, satellite television broadcast units, and bloggers with laptops and smartphones looked out of place on this barren patch of the Atacama Desert. What was there to report from this harsh landscape?

The real story was unfolding beneath them. That's where 33 miners—32 Chileans and one Bolivian—were trapped. Between them and the outside world lay half a mile of solid rock. Beneath that rock layer were the collapsed shafts of the San José copper and gold mine, the last known whereabouts of the miners.

The men had somehow survived the cave-in and managed to alert mine officials above them. But how could rescue teams ever hope to find the men, let alone bring them back to safety? Were all those reporters gathered to report a tragedy or were they—like the rest of the world—hoping for a miracle?

WHAT WENT WRONG?

IN THE EARLY HOURS of August 5, 2010, a new shift of miners started work at the San José Mine, near Copiapó, Chile. Some of the night-shift workers on their way out told them that the mountain had been "weeping" (echoing with the sound of distant collapses) a lot during the night, but things seemed settled again. Men continued to load dump trucks, which would spiral their way up exit tunnels to reach the surface. At 2 p.m., a deafening explosion was followed by a blast of soot and dust from the tunnels. Part of the mine had collapsed, sending the debris out and blocking the exits.

Thirty-three miners were trapped about 2,300 feet down. Somehow they made it through the choking dust to a protected space called the shelter, a special room with a heavy metal door and its own ventilation shaft. They were alive and had emergency food and drink, but there was no way of letting the outside world know.

Meanwhile, rescue workers began drilling holes and sending listening devices down to check for survivors. On August 22, seventeen days after the crash, one of those probes returned to the surface with a note reading (in Spanish), "All 33 of us are well, inside the shelter."

Joy spread among the workers above ground, and soon the miners' predicament turned into an international news story. More food and notes could be sent up and down the emergency ventilation shaft, but it seemed unlikely that the men would ever make it out. The emergency hole was only inches wide.

Yet the men did escape 69 days after the collapse, setting a record for the longest period underground before being rescued. The engineering involved in the rescue called for international cooperation, precise calculations, and luck.

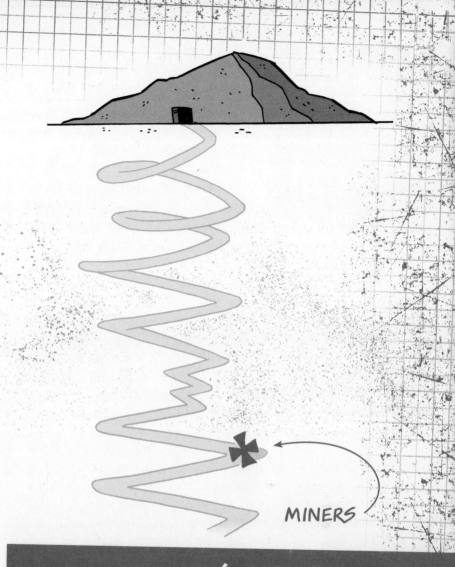

MINERS

THE SAN JOSÉ MINE

The rock of the San José Mine has been giving up its copper and gold since 1889. Miners have used different techniques over the years, ranging from pickaxes and shovels to explosives and conveyor belts. Trucks and other vehicles transport miners inside the mountain, spiraling up and down a four-mile-long central road called the ramp. Passageways lead left and right from the ramp into mining caverns. The deepest of these is more than 2,500 below ground level.

TURN BACK THE CLOCK

DEEP MINING IS A risky operation. Miners and their machinery will work their way into a mountain, extracting the precious metal and ore until it becomes too dangerous to continue in that section of the mine or the quality of the ore declines.

Then it's time to move on, deeper into the mine, with one or more abandoned caverns left behind. The risks continue to build. Miners face dangers with every new seam they mine, but the abandoned caverns come back to haunt them. Without constant propping up, they can collapse, sending choking dust through the mine and blocking air shafts and exit tunnels for the miners beyond.

ORE

A rock containing precious metal.

The layers of rock—ore mixed with harder or softer rock types—themselves can become unstable. The drilling and vibrations from mining vehicles add to that instability; plus, all of Chile lies in a high-risk earthquake zone. A series of small mini-earthquakes, or tremors, can cause a collapse at any moment.

The San José Mine collapse also shows the importance of maintaining strong safety regulations. Mines operated by the Chilean state mining company as well as those owned by international companies have wide-ranging regulations governing them but the San José Mine was a privately owned, smaller mine, and it was known to have less safety

SEAM

An underground layer of precious minerals such as coal, copper, or gold.

equipment. Eight workers had died in the 12 years leading up to the 2010 collapse, and the mine was fined 42 times between 2004 and 2010 for breaking safety rules. When the mine collapsed in 2010, the miners could have escaped from a ventilation shaft that had remained open for two days until another collapse blocked it—except the ladder had been removed!

EMERGENCY SUPPLIES

Until the miners made contact with rescue teams 17 days after the collapse, they had to rely on the emergency supplies of food and drink that were in the shelter. But these supplies were meant to last only two to three days! The miners divided these rations carefully, to make them last. One of the miners recalled how they would have "two little spoonfuls of tuna, a sip of milk, and a biscuit every 48 hours."

STAY ON TARGET

One of the engineering triumphs of the Chilean mine rescue involved sensitive drilling equipment coupled with skilled rescue teams at the top who were able to interpret the information coming up from deep underground. You can get a clear idea of their difficulties—and the sense of triumph when they made contact—with this shoebox demonstration.

It's easy to make and works well as a contest with you and your friends. See who has the most patience—and the most sensitive fingers.

YOU WILL NEED

- Scissors
- Large shoebox with lid
- Small toy magnet
- Metal cooking skewer or other narrow rod (slightly longer than the box)
- Metal hex nut or washer (³⁄₈-inch or ½-inch): make sure the magnet works on it
- Glue
- Mounting putty
- 6 small stones or bits of gravel
- Friends
- Watch or timer

METHOD

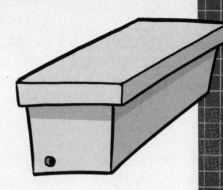

1 Use the scissors to cut a ¾-inch hole in one of the narrow ends of the box, about a quarter of the way across the bottom of the box.

2 Stick the magnet onto one end of the skewer with mounting putty.

3 Place the hex nut (representing a trapped miner) near one of the narrow ends of the box.

4 Slide the skewer through the hole and along the bottom of the box until it reaches the hex nut (which should stick to it).

5 Keeping the skewer and nut in place, glue the stones randomly to the base of the shoebox, but making sure that there's clearance to pull the skewer back out.

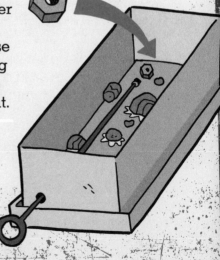

CONTINUED

6 Slowly pull the skewer (with the hex nut on it) back so that you can be sure it will come out with the nut; put the hex nut back inside.

7 Put the lid on the shoebox.

8 Ask a friend to send the exploratory drill (the skewer) into the shoebox mine and to bring the miner out safely. There's a 1-minute limit, to represent the real-life urgency.

9 Let every friend have a turn, making sure that no one sees the pattern of stones if you have to lift the lid. The winner is the person who rescues the miner the fastest.

WHAT'S UP?

The real-life exploratory drills had sensitive listening devices to detect signs of life deep in the mine. Those devices picked up vibrations, either in the air or through the rock, which would register as slight touches on the instrument. A careful "rescuer" in this demonstration should also be able to use their sense of touch, because the click of the hexinut (or washer) being attracted to the magnet is different from the bump when the skewer hits a rock. And those rocks represent the difficulties that the rescuers faced, drilling down through rocks of different thicknesses.

THE METRODOME DEFLATES

Football fans in Detroit got an early Christmas present in 2010: an unexpected Monday night NFL game at Ford Field. But instead of cheering for their home-team Lions, Detroiters watched the rival Minnesota Vikings take on the New York Giants.

No, Santa Claus wasn't playing tricks on them—the Vikings needed a place to play after their home stadium, the Hubert H. Humphrey Metrodome, deflated like a balloon. Two days earlier, a blizzard had dumped 17 inches of snow on Minneapolis, and "The Dome" fell victim. Rain and snow should've just slid right off the roof, but not this time. Despite the efforts of the groundskeepers to hose the roof off with hot water, the snow just collected and the roof collapsed. Cameras inside the stadium captured video of the roof flowing down onto the playing field, already marked for the Vikings game.

After the collapse, one sweet-toothed eyewitness laughingly described the Metrodome as looking "like a bowl of sugar." But it was no laughing matter for the building's owners—or for Vikings fans who had tickets for the Giants game.

WHAT WENT WRONG?

IT'S COMMON FOR stadiums to have a domed roof. Most have rigid supports known as trusses to give them strength. You can see these trusses arching across the open top of a retractable stadium (in which a roof can be opened or closed) or on the outside of a domed roof. But the Metrodome, which opened in 1982, had nothing to hold the dome up. What was going on here? Well, the Dome was supported simply by air. The light, thin (less than 0.05 inch) roof covering resembled the fabric that stretches across trampolines. When the air pressure beneath the fabric was strong and consistent, it would blow up like a balloon.

Unlike a balloon, which will stay inflated once you tie its end, the Dome needed a constant supply of air pushing up on it. Huge electrical fans inside the stadium provided that air supply, and the designers also knew that air would rush out through entrances (like a deflating balloon) unless they took some precautions. They installed revolving doors—giant versions of the sort you might see in a big toy or department store—to help control the flow of air.

Here's where the scientific principles—and trouble—come in. That thin, flimsy roof stays in place as long as the air pressure inside equals or is greater than the force coming down on it on the outside. The Dome's sloping shape should have helped keep those outside pressures down, as well. After all, water would flow right off the roof, and most snow could be blown or even swept off.

But the unexpected happened that December weekend in 2010. Heavy, slushy snow collected and stuck to the roof, creating pockets of extra weight. With that extra pressure pushing down, the fabric tore. Air rushed out of the puncture, reducing the inside air pressure dramatically. And that's when the Dome just crumpled in on itself.

NOT THE FIRST TIME

The Metrodome wasn't the first inflatable stadium to lose pressure and "deflate." The football stadium at the University of Northern Iowa (UNI) was built around the same time as the Metrodome and had collapsed several times before the university replaced it with a rigid structure. Since 2010, many inflatable domes have been demolished or upgraded with supports, like those in St. Louis, Indianapolis, Perth (Australia), Vancouver (Canada), and elsewhere.

TURN BACK THE CLOCK

LET'S CONSIDER why inflatable stadiums were developed in the first place. Sure, you need a lot of fabric to form the roof—the Metrodome, for example, covered 10 acres. But once you've attached it to the perimeter (outer edge) of the stadium, there's no more construction—the air does the rest. The fabric can be almost transparent, letting in more natural light and reducing electrical lighting costs inside. On the whole, it's a lot faster and easier to construct.

These were all attractive ideas back in the early 1970s, when the first inflatable stadiums were being developed. But even before the Metrodome collapse (and others like it), the disadvantages were becoming clear. The most obvious was that fans needed to be running full-time just to keep the roof on. By 2010, the Metrodome operators were paying $60,000 a month for these fans alone!

That flexible, easy-to-inflate roof material also seemed a lot less attractive when people realized that it didn't hold in heat nearly as well as traditional, rigid buildings that are insulated. It costs a pretty penny to heat an inflatable stadium.

INSULATION

Material that can reduce or stop the transfer of heat, sound, or electricity. Heat insulation prevents heat from escaping from a warm area to a colder one.

In 2013, the Minnesota Sports Facilities Authority decided to demolish the Metrodome. The Vikings played their last game there on December 29, 2013. They won 14–13, defeating—appropriately enough—the Detroit Lions.

"PONDING"

Grounds staff at inflatable stadiums try to heat up snow—with hot air or hot water—so that it will run off safely from the roof. Sometimes this runoff backs up, though, and can collect and form pockets (or "ponds") where sections of the fabric meet. These ponds create more stress on the roof and can even tear the fabric and cause collapses.

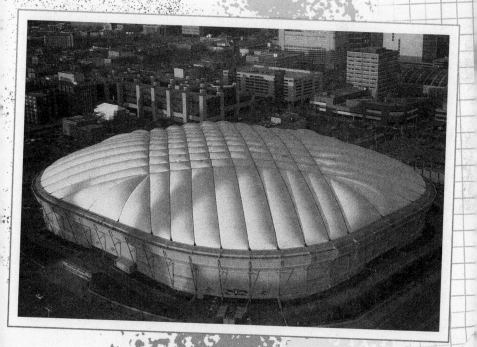

THE PRESSURE'S ON

The whole idea of inflatable stadiums is based on air pressure and its relationship with the pressure pushing in. If the outward pressure from the inside of the stadium (or the balloon in this experiment) is greater or the same as the inward pressure from outside, the structure won't burst. You can see this principle in action, starting with your own mini version of the Metrodome collapse. Remember, it all started at one small tear in its roof—just like the single point of your thumbtack.

YOU WILL NEED

- ➤ Glue
- ➤ 31 thumbtacks
- ➤ Sheet of construction paper
- ➤ Balloons
- ➤ Safety gloves
- ➤ Goggles
- ➤ Friend
- ➤ Small hardback book

TAKE CARE!

You'll be fine if you're careful performing this experiment. But it does involve sharp tacks and balloons that can explode, so make sure to wear those goggles.

METHOD

1 Glue 30 thumbtacks, flat side down, on the construction paper in six rows of five (almost touching each other, and using just a little glue on each).

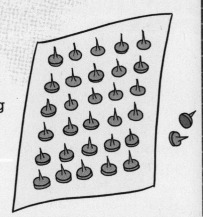

2 Blow up two balloons and put on the safety gloves and goggles.

3 Hold up the remaining thumbtack and ask your friend what will happen if you press the balloon against the point.

4 Carefully press it and watch the balloon pop.

5 Ask your friend what will happen if you rest a balloon on 30 thumbtacks. They might expect an even bigger pop.

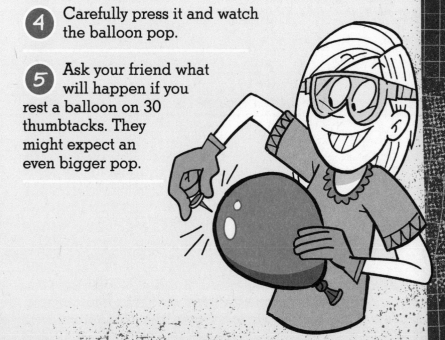

6 Place the second balloon carefully on the thumbtack arrangement, then put the book over it and press down slowly and carefully. It shouldn't burst the balloon.

7 You can continue pressing down, showing how much force you're using.

WHAT'S UP?

Scientists define pressure as the amount of force over an area, or the amount of force *divided by* that area. You pressed in on both balloons with about the same force, but that force was concentrated on a very small area (the point of the thumbtack) with the first balloon— meaning the pressure was high. Dividing that same force over a larger area (the arrangement of 30 thumbtacks) reduced the pressure. The blanket of snow that would normally cover the Metrodome would spread the pressure in just the same way, keeping the stadium inflated. But the concentrated pockets of heavy, wet snow were like large-scale versions of pricking the balloon with just one thumbtack.

WHY A DOME?

One of the reasons why the Metrodome had a dome-shaped roof was to spread the air pressure equally. The dome shape does that very well and can support lots of weight by transferring forces. The Romans were the first people to put this principle into practice: One of their earliest domed buildings, the Pantheon, was built nearly 1,900 years ago and still stands. Its curving, domed roof has no supports apart from its own shape—and it even has a hole at the very top!

The dome shape also occurs in nature, and you'll have a chance to test the strength of one of these yourself. Make sure you do this in the kitchen. You might be having omelets for lunch!

YOU WILL NEED

➤ **Scissors**
➤ **Paper towel**
➤ **3 eggcups**
➤ **3 eggs**
➤ **Table**
➤ **2-gallon plastic container**
   (cylinder-shaped, with flat bottom)
➤ **1-pint measuring pitcher**
➤ **Water**

METHOD

1 Use the scissors to cut up three pieces of paper towel, each about 1½ inches square, and tuck them into the three eggcups (as extra lining).

2 Stand the three eggs in the three eggcups, narrow side up.

3 Set the eggcups on the table in a triangle arrangement, with each side about 3 inches long.

4 Carefully rest the empty container on the eggs, so the eggs are in the center.

5 Fill the pitcher with a pint of water and pour it into the container. The eggs shouldn't break, even though a pint of water weighs a pound.

6 Continue repeating Step 5. Stop after 10 pints or—unlikely—if the eggs break.

WHAT'S UP?

Your eggs can withstand as many as 17 pints of water. That's because a dome takes the basic strengths of an arch—especially its ability to support enormous weight—and uses it in three dimensions. The shape of an arch or a dome allows it to transfer the force of its weight gradually down its curving sides, rather than concentrating all of it in one place, as would happen where a vertical wall met a horizontal support. It also makes it easier to build roomy, high-ceilinged interior spaces. The Metrodome had those height advantages, but the inflatable construction made it less able to withstand outside forces.

THE INFAMOUS "FRYSCRAPER"

The narrow streets of London's financial district often look like forests of umbrellas as stockbrokers and bankers in pin-striped suits dodge puddles in the rain. But stretches of those same streets have recently been scorched by an unlikely source—the sun's rays, concentrated into a burning beam.

The burning ray comes from 20 Fenchurch Street, a mirrored skyscraper rising 37 stories high. Under certain conditions, its curved sides powerfully focus and reflect sunlight downward. It has melted dashboards and peeled paint off vehicles below it, cracked wall tiles of neighboring businesses, and is said to have started fires.

The reflective skyscraper has been nicknamed the "Walkie Scorchie" and "The Fryscraper." But to the building's owners, it's not "jolly good fun." They've already had to pay for damage to property, though thankfully no one's been seriously injured—so far.

WHAT WENT WRONG?

LIKE MOST EUROPEAN cities, London came late to skyscrapers. For centuries, its skyline was dominated by church spires, palace towers, and bridges. After the heavy bombing of London in World War II, a building boom in the 1960s saw modern glass-and-metal buildings popping up everywhere. Even these new buildings, however, were small compared to the towers of New York City, Chicago, or Hong Kong. Things changed in the 1980s when the British government promoted London as an international financial center and relaxed some of the building regulations that were still in place.

One of those regulations had limited the height of new towers, especially those that might overshadow ancient churches and other buildings. So London's "age of skyscrapers" had finally arrived. By this time, skyscraper designs had moved away from the simple "glass rectangle" approach. Modern architects were more playful and creative, tinkering with shapes and adding curves and irregular features. Some of London's newest

GREEK BURNING MIRRORS?

Once news of the "Fryscraper" spread, many people criticized its architect, Rafael Viñoly, for not paying attention to history. The idea of a giant curved mirror reflecting and focusing sunlight into a destructive ray goes back thousands of years. One story has it that the great scientist Archimedes used "burning mirrors" to protect the Sicilian port of Syracuse from Roman attack in 212 BC. These mirrors supposedly reflected the midday sun and caused destructive fires on the Roman ships.

buildings, built in this spirit, have already been nick-named "the Gherkin" (which looks like a giant pickle, or gherkin), "the Shard" (resembling a shard of glass), and "the Cheese Grater," "the Pringle," and "the Can of Ham" (which look like . . . well, you can guess).

The mirror-glass building going up at 20 Fenchurch Street had been known as "the Pint Glass" as it took shape—until shopkeepers and restaurant owners at ground level starting noticing intense light being reflected down from the building in the summer of 2013. The beam burned welcome mats, cracked floor tiles, and melted vehicle dashboards and paintwork.

The "Pint Glass" had transformed into . . . (cue the scary music) . . . "the Fryscraper"! And its designers had to think of some way to stop the problem before it became a real-life "death ray."

TURN BACK THE CLOCK

SUNLIGHT THAT reflects off a concave mirror (like the mirrored sides of the Fryscraper) behaves in much the same way as light passing through a magnifying glass. The technical term for this effect is solar convergence. "Solar," of course, means "relating to the sun." And "convergence" describes things coming together (for instance, thousands of people converge on New York City's Times Square every New Year's Eve).

The sunlight hitting a concave surface doesn't bounce straight back (as it would from, say, a flat bathroom mirror). Instead, the angle makes it bounce both back and slightly *inward* at the same time. The rays of sunlight hitting the different parts of the curve converge at a focal point as they bounce back, and that's where things really heat up. That convergence gives the reflected rays more power. Temperatures of more than 160°F have been reached outside the Fryscraper!

The architect of 20 Fenchurch Street, Rafael Viñoly, wanted the concave shape because it's a graceful way of increasing space on the upper floors, where there's room to jut out beyond the lower buildings. He accepts that the shape and mirrored exterior (designed as a way to keep the building cool inside) create solar convergence—but his computer projections predicted much lower reflected temperatures.

CONCAVE

Description of a shape that curves inward, like a bowl.

That might be the case, but the problem still needs a solution. The owners of the building decided to put a temporary screen on the section of the building that's causing the trouble. Viñoly insists that the permanent awning, installed in 2014 on the south side of the upper floors, has solved the problem.

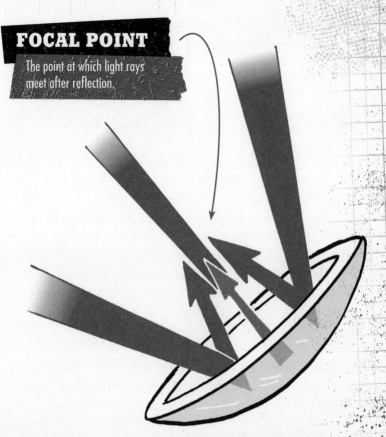

FOCAL POINT
The point at which light rays meet after reflection.

SOLAR CONVERGENCE

LAS VEGAS "HOT SPOT"

Rafael Viñoly seems to be building a hot reputation for himself. He also designed the $8 billion Vdara hotel complex in Las Vegas, Nevada. The Vdara has a concave wall, and in September 2010 it also showed signs of "solar convergence." The Las Vegas sun is much stronger than London's, and the hotel owners were quick to respond when guests complained of burning hair and melting plastic bags down by the hotel pool. They covered the glass with a nonreflective film.

REFLECT OR ABSORB?

The sun travels a different path throughout the year—higher in the summer and lower in the winter—so the angle of reflection also changes. It's really only over the course of several weeks at the start of summer that it causes trouble for the Fryscraper, and during that time the building's owners need to take action. While Viñoly's Vdara Hotel in Las Vegas now has windows coated with a nonreflective film (like permanently wearing a pair of giant sunglasses), the Fryscraper has temporary screens and an awning to shade the offending area.

Here's a chance to remind yourself of what goes on with solar convergence, and then you can test out different remedies. As you might imagine, it works best on a sunny day and in warm weather (but try it anytime).

YOU WILL NEED

> Newspaper
> 4 small stones (optional)
> Magnifying glass
> Water
> Window screening or screen patches (ideally of different mesh sizes)
> Sunglasses

TAKE CARE!

Make sure you do this experiment with adult supervision.

METHOD

1 Tear off a piece of newspaper (about 6 inches square) and place it on the ground, anchored with small stones if it's windy.

2 Hold the magnifying glass above the paper and line it up with the sun.

3 Keeping it at that angle, move the magnifying glass closer to, and farther from, the paper until the circle of light it creates is brightest and smallest.

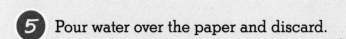

4 Hold the magnifying glass in position until the paper starts to singe, smoke, and then catch fire.

5 Pour water over the paper and discard.

6 Repeat Steps 1 to 5 while holding a screen between the magnifying glass and the paper; continue testing with different screens (if you have them) and then with sunglasses.

7 Record your results.

WHAT'S UP?

The curved surface of the magnifying glass focuses the sun's rays just as the Fryscraper's mirror-glass does. The difference is that the sunlight passes through the magnifying glass and continues onward rather than being reflected. In this experiment, the screen and sunglasses work to scatter the light coming in through the glass so that it won't focus and create the extra energy that burns things. Don't forget, though, that part of the reason for having mirrored walls is to reflect the sunlight to keep the inside of the buildings cool. The owners have to make sure that by stopping the building from reflecting the sunlight, they don't wind up absorbing more and warming up the inside of the building too much.

THE UMBRELLA OVEN

The curved, concave shape of the Fryscraper is sometimes called a parabola. Some umbrellas are also the shape of a parabola, and with a little ingenuity you can turn one into an oven that uses the principle of solar convergence.

Make sure to use an old umbrella that's "on its way out" anyway, because you'll be altering it. An umbrella that opens up into 16 sections works best (it's most like a parabola), but you can try others if that's all you have. Let's get cooking!

YOU WILL NEED

- ➤ **Sunglasses with polycarbonate lenses**
- ➤ **Old umbrella that still opens (4-foot diameter when opened)**
- ➤ **Glue**
- ➤ **Aluminum foil**
- ➤ **Adult**
- ➤ **Metal saw**
- ➤ **Safety gloves**
- ➤ **Fireplace match**
- ➤ **Small, dark-colored pot with lid (optional)**
- ➤ **Tripod plant stand (optional)**

METHOD

1. Make sure everyone is wearing sunglasses.

2. Open the umbrella and put it down so the inside is pointing up.

3. Glue aluminum foil (shiny side out) to the inside of the umbrella; flatten it as you go along, as if it were wallpaper.

4. Ask an adult to saw off the handle, about 5 to 6 inches away from where it meets the center of the umbrella.

5. Place the umbrella on a dry, sunny surface like a sidewalk so that the foil-covered side faces the sun directly.

6. If the umbrella has a pointy tip sticking beyond the outside of it (from what would be the top); the umbrella can rest on that so it's at an angle. If the umbrella lacks that tip, rest it against a piece of wood or a rock to form an angle as it is aimed at the sun.

CONTINUED

7 To test its heating power, ask an adult to wear gloves and hold an unlit fireplace match in front of the "oven."

8 The adult should move the match until it is in the brightest part of the reflected light; he or she should hold it there until it lights (after a few seconds).

9 Optional: For real cooking, prop up the umbrella more, then hold a pot and plant stand over the brightest reflection (just as you did with the match); then cut three holes in the umbrella directly beneath that point so the tripod can rest and the pot can heat up.

WHAT'S UP?

The parabolic shape of the opened umbrella is similar to the concave curves of the Fryscraper and the Las Vegas hotel. The "arms" of the parabola—in this case the curving frame of the umbrella—curve so that all the light is reflected toward one area. An arc, on the other hand, has a constant curvature (because it's part of a circle) and would scatter the bouncing light in different directions. A parabola has the amazing ability to condense light in one area, losing less energy. So with your parabolic umbrella, the reflected sunlight converges into a hot spot, and your food cooks better. The output (heating power) of the oven will depend on several other factors, such as its size, the strength of the sun, and the angle. Can you think of any other factors that might affect it?

AFTERWORD

Before you opened this book, you probably thought twice about walking under ladders, going too high on a swing, or setting off on your bike with worn tires. Now that you've read through these pages, you have a lot more to think about:

Is that the roar of a molasses tsunami that you hear in the distance?

Will this lake drain away if you and your friends go for a swim?

Will you get a sunburn if you walk too close to that skyscraper?

Come to think of it, are those skyscraper windows wobbling a bit—way, way up there?

Some of these risks, of course, are pretty rare and unlikely to affect you. But they do occur, even when trained architects, engineers, and builders have been involved. Of course, you need good tools to build things, but some of the most essential tools are in people's heads—like a grasp of basic engineering principles and common sense.

You'll have to supply your own common sense, but reading this book will have helped you grasp some of those engineering basics that can cause—or prevent—disasters. And the experiments gave you firsthand experience of putting those principles to work in the real world.

Now that you have the tools, it's time to use them with projects of your own. Next stop—the drawing board!

AT A GLANCE

Got a minute to spare? Are you stuck inside on a rainy weekend? Here's a quick rundown of how long the experiments take to get a dramatic payoff.

THE "WOW" FACTOR (LESS THAN 2 MINUTES)

Snap, Crackle 58
Staying Afloat 66
Slow as Molasses? 84
Metal Expansion 198

SNAP TO IT (LESS THAN 5 MINUTES)

Hold That Pose 10
Will It Tip? 34
Flying High 46
Pressure Drop 124

A BIT OF PLANNING (5–15 MINUTES)

From the Ground Up 20
It's Sinking In 36
Overflow! 70
Don't Give Me Static 92
Down in Flames 95
"Drag" Racing 127
Into the Swing 140
Spinning Out 154

Double Hulls 188
Why a Dome? 219
Reflect or Absorb? 228

ON THE HOUR
(UP TO 1 HOUR)

Weighing the Possibilities 24
Holding Up to Pressure 80
Damping Tactics 104
Elephant's Footprint 114
The Violent Vortex 164
Taking Things Wide 174
Onward and Upward 178
Stay On Target 206
The Pressure's On 216

THE DAY SHIFT
(1-8 HOURS)

Wind Load 54
Blowing Hot and Cold 136
The Umbrella Oven 232

PLANNING AHEAD
(A FULL DAY OR MORE)

All Shook Up 6
Corrosion Damage 150

PHOTO CREDITS

GENIUS AT WORK!

More Books by
SEAN CONNOLLY

Sixty-four amazing science experiments that require no special training, use stuff from around the house, and demonstrate scientific principles like osmosis and Newton's Third Law of Motion.

Perform 18 experiments! Includes a book with step-by-step instructions, plus a lateral split-orb measuring spoon, a vacuumatic test tube, a matter-retaining measuring cup, and photon-refracting goggles.

Fifty awesome experiments that allow kids to understand 34 of the greatest scientific break-throughs in history.

Math rocks! At least it does in the gifted hands of Sean Connolly, who blends middle school math with fantasy to create 24 problems that challenge readers on fractions, algebra, geometry, and more.

Fifty-four all-star experiments that demonstrate the scientific principles powering a variety of sports, from why a knuckleball flutters to how LeBron James seems to float through the air on a dunk.